ESSENTIAL
MINI COOPER

ESSENTIAL
MINI COOPER

THE CARS AND THEIR STORY 1961-71 & 1990 TO DATE
• •
ANDERS DITLEV CLAUSAGER

BAY
VIEW
BOOKS
FROM

MBI Publishing Company

This edition first published in 1997 by Bay View Books
Limited, Bideford, Devon, EX39 2PZ England

© Bay View Books Limited, 1997

Published by MBI Publishing Company, 729 Prospect
Avenue, PO Box 1, Osceola, WI 54020-0001 USA

MBI Publishing Company books are also available at
discounts in bulk quantity for industrial or sales-
promotional use. For details write to Special Sales
Manager at Motorbooks International Wholesalers &
Distributors, 729 Prospect Avenue, PO Box 1,
Osceola, WI 54020-0001 USA.

Edited by Mark Hughes
Typesetting and design by Chris Fayers & Sarah Ward

Library of Congress Cataloging-in-Publication Data
Available

ISBN 1-870979-86-9

Printed in China

CONTENTS

FROM MINI TO MINI COOPER

Of all the thousands of different cars manufactured over the last century, only a very few have truly made history. There may only be three such cars which rise above the common herd in the sense that they have brought about major changes to society or to the development of the motor car itself – the Ford Model T, the Volkswagen Beetle and the Mini.

The Model T heralded the start of mass-production and put America on wheels. The Beetle performed a similar role in many European countries and, as the highest-selling car in the world, remains in production after more than 50 years. Yet neither the Model T nor the Beetle would in the long term radically change the way that cars are designed – this was the role of the Mini.

As the first modern car to use a transverse engine and front-wheel drive, the Mini began a revolution that led to almost every other car manufacturer adopting a similar lay-out. It has also had a respectable run as a production car, of 37 years and with a total of over 5.3 million built at the time of writing.

This delightful family picnic scene suggests how BMC saw the Mini, here in Morris form, at the time of its launch in August 1959.

The Mini is now so familiar that it is only too easy to forget exactly how radical it was in 1959. There were few enough front-wheel drive cars on the market, none of them British and none with a transverse four-cylinder engine. The Mini also broke new ground in its compact bodywork, with unequalled use of space: more than 80 per cent of the 10ft (3.05m) overall length was given over to passengers and luggage. It had tiny 10in wheels and all-independent suspension with rubber elements.

The Mini was designed as a small, affordable and economical family car. At just under £500 for the standard version, it was not the cheapest car on the British market, but in every respect it was vastly superior to any competitor. Yet it is not in this intended role that the Mini has had its greatest impact, nor for that matter is it thought of primarily as a torch-bearer for a design

Another feature of the new car was its unheard-of compactness, allowing easy parking in confined spaces. These were the three colours available on Austin Sevens.

Classic early Mini under-bonnet view. The original 848cc engine developed a modest 34bhp.

revolution. Instead, the Mini has become an icon, a car whose personality seems to be more important than what it actually does. To some, a fond memory – 'you never forget your first Mini'. To others, a much loved family member or companion. To well-off women in Tokyo or Düsseldorf, a status symbol and fashion accessory.

If ever any car was all things to all people, the Mini is it. It is a car with a multiple personality of which *The Motor* in 1959 wrote, almost prophetically, 'provided you already have a Mini, a Rolls-Royce makes an ideal second car'. Now, its status as a design classic is assured – a definitive reminder of the 'swinging sixties', a time when Britain was rapidly changing, when British designers in many fields were breaking boundaries, when the England football team won the World Cup, when a Brave New World was peopled by *The Beatles*, Harold Wilson's Labour government, Princess Margaret and Lord Snowdon, Peter Sellers, Mary Quant and Twiggy (many of them Mini owners). The Mini is right up there with the Levis 501s, the Zippo lighter and Ray-Ban sunglasses.

Its functionality and ubiquity has made it the automotive equivalent of the Dr Martens boot. Classless and ageless, it is a car for the dustman as well as the Duchess.

Looked at more dispassionately, the Mini is a car which reflects the preoccupations of its designer, Alec Issigonis (1906-88). Remembered by those who knew him as rather eccentric, both in his personality and his design ideas, Sir Alec (who was knighted in 1969) was born in present-day Turkey, the son of a Bavarian mother and a Greek father who became a naturalised British subject. Together with his widowed mother, he arrived in London in 1923 where he pursued somewhat erratic engineering studies. His working career in the motor industry began in 1928, and in 1936 he joined Morris Motors at Cowley as a suspension draughtsman.

Here his talents found an outlet and his ideas took shape. He was convinced that a front-heavy car with independent suspension offered significant handling advantages. An early suspension design was eventually used on MG cars from 1947 to 1980. In his spare time,

One of the early Mini prototypes, with the engine the other way round, battery in the front and an Austin A35 grille for camouflage.

together with his friend George Dowson, he built the single-seater racing car known as the 'Lightweight Special', notable for its all-independent rubber suspension and monocoque aluminium bodywork. During the war years, he developed a small car design, according to his convictions. This was put on the market in 1948 as the Morris Minor. It became Britain's most successful production car up to that time, with a million sales by 1961 and 1.6 million by 1971. With its engine mounted ahead of the front axle line, independent front suspension with torsion bars, small 14in wheels and unitary construction bodywork in the then-fashionable American idiom, the Minor was as far as Issigonis could go at the time, bearing in mind the innate conservatism of Lord Nuffield and the Morris company.

Issigonis became disillusioned with his prospects after Morris merged with Austin to form BMC in 1952. Before leaving Cowley, he and his small team of assistants did build a front-wheel drive version of the Minor, with a transverse engine. But for the next four years Issigonis was to work for the Alvis company, on a very different type of car – a V8-engined compact luxury sports saloon.

When Alvis decided it could not afford to put this car into production, Issigonis moved back into the BMC fold, now setting up shop in the Austin factory at Longbridge where he found a patron in the shape of BMC's chairman, Leonard Lord.

After an exercise designing a medium-sized family saloon, the XC 9001, which was to bequeath its uncompromising body styling to the Mini and whose suspension eventually became the Hydrolastic system, Issigonis was given a specific task by Lord – to design a proper small car, 'to drive the bubble cars off the road' in the wake of the Suez crisis of 1956, which had caused petrol rationing to be introduced in Britain, and thus given the 'bubble cars' a short-lived fillip. The only constraint was that the new small car must use an existing BMC engine.

In what by modern standards seems an incredibly short time, with a small team of hand-picked and trusted

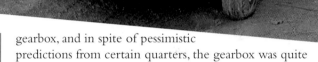

On test in the spring of 1959, this pre-production Mini has the fixed grille later used on the van and pick-up models. The driver is Jack Daniels, Issigonis's right-hand man.

George Harriman, BMC's managing director, and Alec Issigonis inspect one of their new babies at Longbridge soon after the launch of the Mini in August 1959.

assistants, and without very much in the way of a budget, Issigonis developed the Mini. The dimensions were arrived at by deciding the minimum size of car that would seat four people and accommodate some luggage. The tiny 10in wheels were adopted from the German bubble cars, while the all-independent rubber suspension was perhaps inspired by the 'Lightweight Special' and was developed by Issigonis's great friend and collaborator, Dr Alex Moulton. The transverse engine position and front-wheel drive came from the earlier Morris Minor prototype, of which Issigonis's assistant Jack Daniels, now a member of the Mini team, had vivid and fond memories. A new element in the equation was Issigonis's idea of putting the gearbox in the sump, the ultimate space-saving measure that permitted fitting BMC's four-cylinder A-series engine transversely within the confines of a narrow front track. It necessitated the use of an intermediary gearwheel between the engine and the

gearbox, and in spite of pessimistic predictions from certain quarters, the gearbox was quite happy to share the engine oil.

Front-wheel drive required constant velocity universal joints which were eventually supplied by Hardy Spicer to the design of the Czech-American inventor Rzeppa – they had been used more than 20 years earlier on the famous Cord 810/812. It also soon turned out that it would be advantageous to mount the power unit, together with front suspension and steering, on one subframe, and the rear suspension on a second subframe, a scheme that helped to prevent engine torque reactions, and road shocks, from being transmitted to the main bodyshell. Body construction was an essay in simplicity, with the famous external welding seams making it possible to employ unskilled labour and use simpler jigs. Every panel seemed to perform a double duty: inner door panels and rear quarter stiffeners became cubbyholes, the scuttle became a parcel shelf, and the boot lid became a luggage carrier.

During 1958 a prototype was ready for BMC chairman Len Lord to drive around the factory. Within five minutes he told Issigonis to put the car into production – within a year. When the startled designer replied that it would cost a lot of money, Lord told him, 'Don't worry, I'll sign the cheques'. And so it happened. The first Austin-badged production car was built, largely by hand by foreman Albert Green at Longbridge in April 1959, with the first Morris-badged car following at Cowley in early May. On 26 August, the new BMC twins – the Austin Seven and the Morris Mini-Minor – were launched.

At first, the world at large reacted with disbelief. Was

this car an elaborate joke? How could a British motor manufacturer, hitherto known for cautious conservatism, possibly have managed to produce what looked to be such a revolutionary car? Would anyone buy this ridiculously small car?

There were not many customers at first – BMC produced less than 20,000 in 1959. Three years later, however, the company turned out more than ten times as many in one year, and kept on doing so for the next 15 years. The Mini quickly asserted itself, and many disbelievers became enthusiastic converts. Its inherent qualities were obvious – the roominess for its size, the road-holding and handling, the manoeuvrability, and the high level of primary safety.

As for performance – well, the original 848cc models had a modest 34bhp to propel an unladen weight of 1300lb (590kg). The top speed was around 73mph (117kph) and 0-60mph (0-96kph) took over 26sec, but the 30-50mph (48-80kph) sprint in third could be accomplished in 10sec. Typical fuel consumption was in the order of 40mpg (around 7 litres per 100km).

There were standard and de-luxe versions of both the Austin and the Morris, differences mostly relating to the quality of interior trim, with cloth upholstery and rubber mats on the £497 standard model, while the £537 de-

luxe model offered two-tone vinyl upholstery, carpets and a bit more in the way of equipment. Each marque offered a choice of three colours, different on Austin and Morris, but in both cases red, blue and white (or light grey). Otherwise the only brand differences were radiator grilles and badges.

With the Mini established in production and gaining increasing acceptance in the marketplace, when exactly did the Mini Cooper begin its gestation? Very soon after the launch of the Mini, it occurred to quite a few different people that the new baby car had the potential of becoming a worthy competition machine. As early as September 1959, the first Minis were entered in rallies, with BMC's own Competitions Department very much in the vanguard.

Marcus Chambers, no less, took an Austin Seven on the Norwegian Viking Rally that September (to finish a lowly 51st overall), while in the following month Pat

The interior of the Mini Cooper development car. The multi-instrument pack, remote control gear lever and door handles are familiar – but the trim looks very strange!

A pensive-looking Alec Issigonis with John Cooper, considering the merits of the LIghtweight Special, on display at a 1960s Racing Car Show.

Moss and Stuart Turner used a Morris Mini-Minor to win the British national rally called the 'Mini Miglia' – a singularly appropriate name. Daniel Richmond of Downton Engineering got hold of an early Austin Seven (registered UHR 850) which he tuned and entered in saloon car racing. Other tuners familiar with the A-series engine, such as Alexander and John Sprinzel of Speedwell, began to take an interest.

Another early Austin Seven, chassis number A-A2S7/589 built in July 1959 and originally allocated to BMC's publicity department, where it was registered YOK 250 and used for the Mini's press launch, was soon lent to John Cooper of The Cooper Car Company Limited. From his premises at Surbiton in Surrey, Cooper made his company one of Britain's leading racing car constructors, winning the drivers' and manufacturers' Formula 1 World Championships in 1959 and 1960 (the driver both years was Jack Brabham). In 1959 Cooper also became the first British constructor to build a single-seater racing car for the new International Formula Junior. This was originally an Italian idea for a low-cost starter formula in racing and demanded the use of a mass-production 1-litre engine. Italian FJ cars used Fiat engines, but Cooper chose to base his racing engine on the BMC A-series.

Cooper's involvement with BMC, therefore, was just starting when the Mini appeared on the scene. The Mini that he was lent by BMC was used for a hurried trip to the Italian Grand Prix at Monza in September 1959, driven there by racing driver Roy Salvadori. While the car was at Monza, Aurelio Lampredi, the Ferrari design engineer who had recently joined Fiat, saw it and asked if he could try it. John Cooper has told the story about Lampredi returning the Mini, saying this was the car of the future – 'if it weren't so ugly, I'd shoot myself!'.

At around this time Cooper had done some work on a rear-engined Renault Dauphine, fitting a Climax engine, with a view to marketing the resulting confection as a performance road car. This was not such a daft idea as it may now seem – the French tuner Amédée Gordini (know as 'le sorcier') had gone to work on the Dauphine in 1957, and one of these cars had won the 1958 Monte Carlo Rally. For some time, the Dauphine Gordini was a force to be reckoned with in European motor sport. However, rear-engined cars have their limitations as regards handling, and the Dauphine's large but lightweight four-door body was not particularly strong.

Instead, the project for a Cooper road car was re-cast with the Mini in the starring role. Cooper approached Issigonis with his idea for a Mini-based Grand Touring

Austin and Morris versions of the Mini Cooper being flagged off at the press launch of the new models in 1961. Launched at the same time as the Mini Coopers (below) were the look-alike Super versions of the Minis – sharing some of the Coopers' cosmetic features but with special grilles, and mechanicals unchanged from standard Minis.

car but was not given the slightest encouragement: Issigonis was totally uninterested in turning his people's car into a racer. Cooper asked him if he had ever taken a Mini round a race track. Issigonis's reply was typical: 'No. Should I have done?' – notwithstanding the fact that in a 'demonstration' at the British Grand Prix at Silverstone in 1960 all the leading racing drivers of the day put Minis through their paces, with Issigonis seemingly an enthusiastic spectator…

Back at Surbiton, 'Ginger' Devlin of Cooper set about tuning a Mini, probably still that early car, YOK 250, which was to remain on the BMC fleet until 1966, presumably spending its time with Cooper. The result was a car which allegedly had three times the power of a standard Mini, in other words about 100bhp. It was also fitted with special small 7in Lockheed disc brakes.

Having been turned down by Issigonis, John Cooper went to the top, to BMC's managing director George Harriman (who in 1961 succeeded Len Lord as chairman of the company). After a test drive in the prototype, Harriman agreed to build 1000 of the cars – the number required for homologation purposes – although he doubted whether BMC could sell that many. He also offered John Cooper a royalty of £2 for each Mini Cooper built. With the minimum of fuss or formalities, agreement was reached between the two men, and BMC took on the development of the production car. To distinguish the Mini Cooper from the basic car, it was given a new project number – ADO 50 rather than the ADO 15 number of the ordinary Mini.

There was, of course, some influence from the BMC-Cooper Formula Junior engine on the Mini Cooper engine, but they were not directly related. The Formula

Junior had started out as a much-tuned 948cc unit, the standard capacity of the A-series at the time, but for the 1961 Cooper FJ Mark II Eddie Maher of BMC's engine factory in Coventry developed a 994cc version. This was bored out from 62.9mm to 64.4mm but kept the normal stroke of 76.2mm. It also ran with a compression ratio of 11.5:1. For the Mini Cooper production car, it was thought desirable to preserve the good torque characteristics of the A-series, yet it was calculated that power would have to be increased to 55bhp for a top speed of 85mph (137kph). Maher, therefore, settled for a much longer stroke of 81.28mm but actually reduced the bore fractionally from the 848cc engine – it came down from 62.94mm to 62.43mm. The resulting capacity was 997cc, neatly below the 1-litre class limit for motor sport. BMC at the time stated that the engine dimensions were 'related to a degree of rationalisation of engine strokes which is planned for future power units' – but in fact no other A-series engine ever used that precise stroke of the 997cc unit. In 1962 the 1098cc unit went up to 83.72mm while the later 1275cc engine had a stroke of 81.33mm…

With the capacity increase came bigger inlet valves,

An early Morris Mini Cooper (top) which was part of the original company press fleet at Cowley. One secret of the space utilisation of the Mini was the combined gearbox and final drive in the sump. The Cooper was the first model to feature this remote control gearchange.

increased in size from 1.093in (27.76mm) to 1.156in (29.36mm). The compression ratio was raised to 9.0:1 although a low-compression version of the Mini Cooper engine (found predominantly on some export models) kept the 8.3:1 compression ratio of the standard Mini. There were two SU HS2 carburettors of 1.25in diameter. The camshaft gave a greater total valve opening, up from 230° to 252°, with an overlap of 37° rather than 15°. With changes also to the combustion chambers and the exhaust system, the result was a power output of the desired 55bhp at 6000rpm, while maximum torque was 54.5lb ft (7.53mkg) at 3600rpm.

Other engine modifications included a stiffer cylinder block and crankcase, while the crankshaft had thicker webs. The main bearings were reduced in width but this was compensated for by the use of lead-bronze bearings which had a higher load capacity than the white metal bearings of ordinary Minis. There was a torsional damper fitted to the nose of the crankshaft, and stiffer (but still single) valve springs. As far as the transmission was concerned, the indirect gear ratios were raised by about 12 per cent but the final drive ratio was 3.765:1, as found on the 848cc models. The gearchange was now from a short remote control lever, of a type that would only be introduced on basic Minis with the 1000 model in 1967. The remote control was a great improvement on the 'soup stirrer' of the other early Minis.

The major change to the running gear was the provision of the 7in Lockheed disc brakes at the front. Very early cars had a brake intensifier or booster, but this was discontinued in early 1962 in favour of a revised master cylinder and brake pedal linkage. The suspension was exactly the same as on the ordinary Minis. The wheels were the same size and type, but the tyres were the latest type of Dunlop Gold Seal, with a nylon casing, size 5.20-10.

As far as the bodywork was concerned, the basic body was unchanged but a few small changes were enough to justify the Cooper versions being given their own series of body numbers (see page 77). The chief points to note were that the Cooper bodies had a new cut-out for the remote control gear lever, with a blanking plate over the hole for the normal gear lever; they did not have the hole for the floor-mounted starter button as the Coopers always had a key-operated starter; and there were additional brackets in the boot for a new carpeted boot floor above the spare wheel and battery. The last two features were shared with the new Super versions of the Minis, introduced at the same time as the Coopers, of which more below.

Externally, the Cooper models had their own unique radiator grilles, different on Austin and Morris, with eleven narrow slats on the Austin and seven broader slats on the Morris. Badges were new, with the Austin Cooper or Morris Cooper legends on the bonnet badge as well as on the boot lid. The bumpers had overriders, supplemented by tubular bumper guards on the front and rear quarters. There was a range of two-tone colour schemes, with the roof in contrasting black or white (see page 77 for a detailed list).

The interior trim was also in two-tone schemes, with the silver/grey or gold/grey so-called 'brocade' material used for seat centres and other trim panels on some cars. The carpet was of a better quality than normal on Minis, and sound deadening was improved. There was an instrument binnacle with three dials, the 100mph (or 160kph) speedometer with its built-in fuel gauge being flanked by smaller dials for water temperature and oil

An early Austin Seven Cooper on test at the MIRA proving ground, together with a contemporary Austin Seven Countryman. Fresh from receiving his knighthood in 1969 (below), Sir Alec Issigonis found time to have his picture taken with his most famous creation.

pressure. Other improvements included chrome-plating for the steering column bracket and the gear lever.

Many of the external cosmetic features and the interior trim, including the instrument pack, were shared by the Austin Super Seven and Morris Mini-Minor Super, which were introduced at the same time as the Cooper models. However, these Supers had different grilles, in the case of the Austin a unique grille with vertical bars supplementing the horizontal wavy-line bars of the standard car, whereas the Morris simply had a chrome version of the normal Morris grille. In this form, the Supers were visually all but indistinguishable from the

Coopers, but they were clearly inferior in terms of performance because they shared the 34bhp 848cc engine of the standard models. They lasted only about a year in production before being 'merged' with the de-luxe versions of the Mini to make the grandly-titled Super-de-Luxe models, which soon after lost the two-tone colour schemes and their Cooper-style interiors. It may be noted that a genuine Super Seven or Mini-Minor Super is now a good deal rarer than any Mini Cooper…

It is worth quoting the relative prices for the different Mini models in October 1961, after the launch of the Mini Cooper and Super models, as well as of the ultimate luxury versions of the Mini, the Riley Elf and Wolseley Hornet. Prices in the UK, including Purchase Tax, were as follows:

Austin or Morris Mini, standard model	£526
Austin or Morris Mini, de-luxe model	£568
Austin Super Seven or Morris Mini-Minor Super	£592
Wolseley Hornet	£672
Riley Elf	£694
Austin or Morris Mini Cooper	£679

It will be seen that a fairly clear pecking order had been established, with the Coopers as well as the Riley being at the top of the price list for those who were prepared to pay extra for either luxury trimmings or performance. The twain did not meet, although the Coopers with their improved trim came closer to providing the best of both worlds. The Riley, for all its wood and leather trim, scarcely lived up to the sporting traditions of its marque, being distinctly lethargic as it originally had only the 34bhp 848cc engine of the ordinary Mini. The Elf was aimed at the distaff side, as a fashion accessory with appeal to woman buyers. The performance-orientated Coopers were, by contrast, aimed mostly at men.

THE MINI COOPER (1961-69)

Launched on 20 September 1961, the Mini Coopers were accompanied by a typical BMC press release illustrated by the famous motoring cartoonist Brockbank, whose sketches showed – perhaps only slightly fancifully – the Mini Cooper seriously hassling a variety of high-performance European cars, including Alfa Romeo, Mercedes-Benz and Porsche – and even a road racing Ferrari!

Early press road tests were highly enthusiastic. *The Motor*, testing the Morris version, headed its report with the description 'A Wolf Cub in Sheep's Clothing' and went on to state: 'This is the fastest production saloon car of its size ever to figure in our regular series of Road Test Reports'. *The Autocar*, at the time the more sober of the weekly magazines, contented itself with the statement that 'the Austin Cooper becomes an astonishingly fast means

This Surf Blue car is a splendidly-preserved example of the original 997cc Morris Mini Cooper, built soon after the September 1961 launch.

of reaching B from A…as road space becomes more and more at a premium, small extra-performance cars like the Austin Cooper will be in increasing demand'. John Bolster in *Autosport* spoke of 'Grand Touring on a Budget', while Bill Boddy in *Motor Sport* used the word 'sensational' and added that 'The performance is quite staggering…one of the quickest A-to-B vehicles I have experienced and an admirable town-car'.

All commentators were united in their praise for the Mini Cooper's combination of performance with tractability and (relative) refinement. The basic excellence of the Mini's road-holding and handling was well up to

15

coping with the 50 per cent increase in power, while the front disc brakes and the close-ratio gearbox with its remote control also came in for praise.

The Autocar measured a best one-way top speed of 87.4mph (140kph) as against the 87mph that BMC claimed for the car, but a more realistic figure was about 85mph (137kph). Acceleration from 0-60mph (0-96kph) took about 17-18sec, while a mere 8sec were necessary to get from 30-50mph (48-80kph) in third gear. Overall fuel consumption figures between 27 and 35mpg (10.6 to 8.2 litres per 100km) were recorded. This would give a worst-case range of only 150 miles (240km) from the standard single fuel tank of 5.5 imperial gallons (25 litres), and it is interesting to note that the car tested by *The Autocar* was already fitted with the extra, right-hand fuel tank, doubling capacity. The second tank otherwise only became available as a regular option in 1963, and then only on the Cooper S models.

As originally launched, the cars were known as the Austin Seven Cooper and Morris Mini-Cooper, notwithstanding the fact that the badges, front and rear, simply read Austin Cooper and Morris Cooper. However, at the beginning of 1962 the Seven name was dropped by Austin, and the basic car became the Austin Mini. Right from the start, the cars were universally known as Mini Coopers, the hyphen dropping out of common usage.

The reason why there had to be two versions was that in the UK, and in many export markets, Austin and Morris still had largely separate dealer networks, although the higher production figures often achieved by Morris versions (see pages 75-76) indicate a preference for the Morris badge abroad. Only Morris-badged versions were marketed in Australia, while most cars in the USA seem to have been Austins.

Whatever the marque badge, all Coopers were built in the Austin factory at Longbridge, and had chassis numbers allocated in batches out of the main Austin Mini number series, typically with 50 numbers (or a multiple thereof) set aside for either Austins or Morrises. No Mini Cooper was ever made in the Morris factory at Cowley, nor was the Cooper racing car factory at Surbiton in any way involved in the production process.

There was, however, Cooper production in other countries, where BMC had set up local assembly operations to circumvent tariff barriers or to simplify shipping, fed with CKD (Completely Knocked Down) kits from Longbridge. Thus, Minis – including Mini Coopers – were assembled round the world in locations varying from Eire to New Zealand. Some of these assembly operations gradually took on the nature of local

manufacturing, and some of these foreign Mini Cooper versions are discussed in a later chapter (see page 53).

Production at Longbridge had actually got under way in July 1961 in preparation for the launch, and George Harriman's pessimism about the sales potential was quickly put to shame. By the end of 1961 almost 1800 cars had been made, and during 1962 nearly 14,000 Coopers were produced (for detailed figures, see pages 75-76). There were few important modifications made to the 997cc cars during their production run, which lasted a little over two years, to the end of 1963. At an early stage, in February 1962, the original brake booster was deleted, while an improved master cylinder and brake linkage were introduced. Two months later new front seats of the single diaphragm type were fitted, with slight revisions to the seat pattern, while in July 1962 the original cone-type synchromesh was replaced by the stronger baulk-ring synchromesh. This most welcome improvement was common to all Minis.

Unlike ordinary Minis at the time, Coopers were fitted with a heater as standard. Early cars had a simple re-circulation type heater, although a more efficient fresh-air type was available as an option. In March 1963 a new type of fresh-air heater was introduced as standard on all cars, except those few export models (destined for hot climates) where it was omitted. At around the same time, there were further revisions to the brake system. In May 1963 the original chrome-plated window catches were replaced by plastic catches, and the number of settings for the catches was reduced. A month later the original individual gauze-type pancake air filters were replaced by the single twin-box air cleaner typical of all later Coopers until 1971.

While the early 997cc Cooper was entered in competitions (see page 38), after the introduction of the Mini Cooper S in 1963 the lesser model increasingly played second fiddle, in the world of motor sport as well as in popular imagination. Nevertheless, the standard model continued to sell steadily, and at the end of 1963 was fitted with a new 998cc engine. This was not actually all that new an engine as it had been used, in single-carburettor form, in the Riley Elf and Wolseley Hornet Mark II models for the best part of a year.

The 998cc engine combined the old A-series stroke of 76.2mm (found on 803cc and 948cc versions) with the 64.58mm bore of the 1098cc version. It was certainly a reasonable way of rationalising the somewhat bewildering selection of A-series engines then in production. In the twin-carburettor form adopted for the Mini Cooper, power output increased from the 38bhp of the

Under the bonnet of a 1961 car, with the small separate air cleaners which were soon replaced by a joint box air cleaner. All Mini Coopers offered rather better sound insulation than the ordinary Minis.

From the rear, this 1961 car is identified simply as a Morris Cooper, badging common to all the Mark I models.

The Mini Cooper soon became sought-after by the rich and famous. This car (left) was supplied to Princess Grace of Monaco. Acting as HRH's stand-in is Pauline Bowler of the Austin Publicity Department at Longbridge. Half a million (below left) is still a respectable production figure. It was reached by the Mini in December 1962, the landmark car being an Austin Mini Cooper, photographed when it came off the Longbridge assembly line.

fraction under 15sec, while the 30-50mph (48-80kph) time in third was down to 7sec. The revised model was launched, rather out-of-season and in a low-key manner, in January 1964, when its price was £568 – the same as the 997cc (after a reduction of Purchase Tax).

Some changes were soon being made to the 998cc model, and most of these also applied to the Mini Cooper S in its different versions. In March 1964 the new Dunlop SP41 radial tyres were fitted as standard, making the Mini Cooper one of the first British production cars to use radial tyres exclusively, only a matter of months after the launch of the Rover 2000, the first car to be so equipped. In April the original Smoke Grey/White colour scheme was replaced by Tweed Grey/White, and a diaphragm spring clutch was introduced. Only two months later, the original 998cc engine (type 9FA) was replaced by a revised engine (type 9FD) which featured positive crankcase ventilation. In the autumn of 1964, a number of comfort and safety features were changed: the cars were fitted with door-mounted courtesy switches for the interior lamp, sun visors became the crushable safety type, and a new rear-view mirror with a plastic frame and backing was introduced.

Elf/Hornet engine to 55bhp, identical to the 997cc engine, but the shorter stroke greatly reduced piston speed and made the new engine a more robust and reliable unit. There was a definite improvement in torque, which rose from 54.5lb ft to 57lb ft (7.88mkg), developed at a usefully lower 3000rpm. Double valve springs were now fitted.

The net result was that the 998cc version produced a small but useful improvement in performance. Top speed was up to 89mph (143kph), with a genuine 90mph available in slightly favourable circumstances. The 0-60mph (0-96kph) sprint could be accomplished in a

The BMC publicity department went to the trouble of arranging a photo shoot in the South of France with left-hand drive cars, using a variety of continental number plates. This is the 'German' Mini Cooper. Sure, the cars were popular all over Europe! Minis were fitted with Hydrolastic suspension (left) in 1964, with these extra coil helper springs at the rear on Coopers.

More importantly, September 1964 saw the biggest change during the production career of the Mini Mark I when the original solid rubber cone suspension was replaced by Hydrolastic suspension on saloon models. This used a pressurised fluid-filled hydraulic displacer unit at each wheel, interconnected front to rear on either side. In addition, there were extra helper coil springs at the rear, but the separate shock absorbers were discontinued because Hydrolastic is self-damping. Hydrolastic had been developed principally by Alex Moulton for the BMC 1100 of 1962, and the Hydrolastic-suspended 1800 was just about to be launched when the system was fitted to the Mini range in 1964. The Hydrolastic elements were manufactured by Dunlop and were always quite expensive, mainly because they needed to be made to very close tolerances.

In the Mini, so much smaller than other Hydrolastic cars, the main advantage was that the system gave a more comfortable ride, by reducing pitch movements, although bounce movements and roll were increased. The ride was still firm, and the car was subject to more pronounced changes in pitch attitude when accelerating or braking. The court remained out on the question of whether or not Hydrolastic was an improvement on the Mini: BMC's own rally team and many other competition-minded drivers preferred the old-style solid suspension. When, in 1969, most Minis reverted to rubber cone suspension, it was probably more for reasons of cost than any factor to do with driveability…

Soon after the new suspension arrived, an improved radiator was fitted, but then there was comparatively quiet on the development front for quite some time. In the

autumn of 1965 the original Surf Blue colour was
replaced by Island Blue, and the fairly unpopular Fiesta
Yellow/White colour scheme was discontinued.
Improved quality carpet was fitted to the cars, while
reclining front seats became available as an optional extra.
In January 1966 home market cars were fitted with sealed
beam headlamps, and new curved door handles with a
safety boss on the door were introduced. Among the last
major improvements was that a heated rear window became
available as an option in November 1966, and a double-
skinned boot lid was introduced in December 1966.

The best production year for the 998cc model was
1966, with almost 15,000 cars delivered. Despite
increasing competition in the small sports saloon car
market, the Mini Cooper could well hold its own.

The delicately-coloured interior of a 1963 model in Powder Blue and grey 'brocade' material. Extra instruments were found on all Coopers, but the 100mph speedometer identifies this as a 997cc (or 998cc) car.

Another distinguishing feature of the Cooper versions was the carpeted boot board, which lifted up to reveal a perfectly ordinary Mini spare wheel and battery with typical cardboard cover.

Ford offered the Anglia Super fitted with the Cortina's 1200cc engine, a fairly tame 48bhp unit which in the smaller car gave a top speed of 82mph (132kph) at a cost of £575 in 1964. Rootes took the basic Hillman Imp and, using true-to-type badge engineering, developed the Singer Chamois in 1964 with the standard 875cc 39bhp engine. Two years later this became the Chamois Sport with all of 42bhp, while also in 1966 there was the Sunbeam Imp Sport with a better 51bhp, still from the unchanged 875cc capacity. At £665 it was more expensive than the £600 asked for the 998cc Cooper. It was also 200lb (91kg) heavier and acceleration was markedly slower, although top speed was a respectable 89mph (143kph). Overall, the Sunbeam Imp and the Mini Cooper were an even match, but the Imp won

easily over the Cooper when it came to comfort – and, in the eyes of many contemporary observers, also on styling.

The boxy little Vauxhall Viva HA, current from 1963 to 1966, was available with a tuned 54bhp engine in its 90 and SL90 versions but these ran out of steam at 82mph (132kph). The better-looking, coke-bottle shaped Viva HB had an 1159cc engine with 69bhp in its 90 version, and another 10bhp when breathed on by Jack Brabham. The 1600cc Viva GT and the 2-litre version only followed later.

Of all the other British small-car manufacturers at the time, Triumph took the most interesting alternative approach. By fitting a 1.6-litre six-cylinder engine in the Herald in 1962, they created the Triumph Vitesse, which had 70bhp at its disposal. With a top speed of 88mph (142kph) and a 0-60mph (0-96kph) time of just under 18sec, performance was surprisingly similar to the 997/998cc Mini Cooper, reflecting the fact that the car weighed 2000lb (908kg) rather than the 1300lb (590kg) of the small BMC car. The Vitesse offered greater comfort and more refinement, with about the same interior room as the Mini but rather more luggage space. At £837 for the saloon model at launch in 1962, it was appreciably more expensive than the Mini Cooper, and appealed to a rather different clientele. The later Vitesse 2-litre could top 95mph (153kph) and went from 0-60mph (0-96kph) in 12.6sec, in other words performance approaching the Mini Cooper S in 1275cc form, and it did not cost all that much more, at £839 compared with £791 for the 1275 S, in October 1966. Anything else in Britain which came anywhere near 100mph performance was either an impractical two-seater sports car or cost more than £1000 – or both.

Of the European competition, the Mini Cooper's arch rival in rallying was the SAAB 96. The Sport version, also variously known as the GT or Monte Carlo model, offered 57bhp and 90mph (145kph) from its 841cc three-cylinder two-stroke engine but was considerably more expensive even than the Mini Cooper S, costing in Switzerland no less than 11,750 Swiss Francs in 1964 compared with Sfr 6750 for a Mini Cooper or Sfr 9200 for the Cooper S. More comparable on price were the Fiat-Abarth models based on the Fiat 500 and 600 models, available in a bewildering variety. The contemporary joke was that the Stage 1 Abarth tuning of a Fiat 500 consisted of a red stripe painted down the side of the car. However, the 600-based 1000 Berlina offered a respectable 96mph (155kph) top speed at a cost of Sfr 9550, putting it firmly in the Mini Cooper S bracket.

Perhaps closest in spirit to the Mini Cooper were the

There is little enough to distinguish a Mini Cooper 998cc engine from any other Mini engine, the twin carburettors apart. This is the later version with positive crankcase ventilation. Obviously the 'Austin' or 'Morris' label on the rocker cover was only added *after* engines were installed in cars. From the rear, the twin carburettors show up better, and the straight-through exhaust manifold can be seen.

sporting TT and TTS versions of the NSU Prinz 1000, current from 1965 to 1972. These intriguing cars had an overhead camshaft air-cooled in-line four-cylinder engine mounted transversely between the rear wheels. The TT model had an 1177cc engine developing 65bhp and a top speed of 95mph (153kph), the competition-orientated TTS a smaller 996cc unit of 70bhp, good for 99mph (160kph). In 1968 a Swiss buyer would have paid Sfr 7980 for the TT or Sfr 9580 for the TTS, at a time when the 998cc and 1275cc S models of the Mini Cooper Mark II cost Sfr 6950 and Sfr 9660 respectively in that market. These NSUs left behind a legend in continental saloon car racing and rallies but were sadly destined for the chop after the company was taken over by Volkswagen and merged with Audi. They remain little-known outside Germany.

The Mini Cooper Mark II..............

In October 1967 BMC finally – after eight years – came around to introducing Mark II versions of the Minis, having made something like 1.6 million of the original models.

Many important modifications had been introduced more or less as running changes, but there had been no attempt at even the most modest stylistic facelift. This was finally implemented on the Mark II but, even so, the changes were remarkably modest. All Mini saloons now had new radiator grilles which were slightly squared off, there was a marginally wider rear window, and the rear light units became larger and more rectangular. Inside was a revised trim package, a new design of steering wheel, and a multi-function stalk switch on the steering column which incorporated headlamp dip and horn operations. All these changes were incorporated on the Mini Cooper. On these Mark II models, Austin and Morris versions had the same radiator grille, with eight

The Mini Cooper Mark II – this is probably an Austin – with the new grille and rear lights, but note that the car has lost the tubular bumper corner guards.

horizontal slats, and the top part of the grille surround was now attached to the bonnet. Badges were new, featuring plastic inserts in chrome bezels. Because of the bigger rear light units, the additional corner bumper guards were discontinued. Mini Coopers now had exactly the same trim as the Super-de-Luxe versions of the ordinary Minis, and apart from a few early cars which had trim colour-coded to the exterior, the only trim colour was a basic black. The carpet was of improved quality, with hessian-backed wool material.

In the Mini Mark II range, the single-carburettor 998cc engine as found on the Elf and Hornet models became available also in the basic Austin and Morris Minis, and these cars now had a remote control gearchange similar to the Mini Cooper, although the Cooper still had its unique chrome-plated gear lever as a special feature – apart of course from the close-ratio gearbox and more powerful twin-carburettor engine. There were very few mechanical changes on the Mark II but it is worth mentioning that a new steering rack was fitted, which helped to reduce the turning circle from the 37ft (11.3m) of the Mark I to a much more reasonable 28ft (8.5m).

The Mark II version of the Mini Cooper 998cc was to have only a short production run, lasting just a little over two years until the model was discontinued in November 1969. Some changes were still made to the car, most notably the much-delayed introduction of a fully-synchronised gearbox in October 1968. Engines fitted with this gearbox may be identified by a new engine number prefix – 9FD-XE-H instead of 9FD-SA-H. Only a few months later, engine number prefixes were more radically altered to bring them into line with a new BMC system, so from March 1969 the 998cc Cooper engines became type 99H-377-C-H if fitted with a dynamo, or type 99H-378-C-H if fitted with an alternator. Alternators had originally been introduced in Britain in the early 1960s and were at first predominantly found on Police cars which required higher current-generating capacity to cope with their additional electrical equipment. The first Mini Coopers to have alternators were also Police vehicles but gradually alternators became more common and by 1969 were fitted to increasing numbers of civilian vehicles.

After BMC had merged with Leyland in early 1968, a far more radical overhaul of the Mini range got under way. The new management of the merged company, with Donald (later Lord) Stokes as its chairman, was determined to rationalise the entire British Leyland model range, and in particular to get rid of BMC's badge engineering. Thus, in 1969, the Riley and Wolseley versions of the Mini disappeared, and it was planned that other Minis should lose the Austin and Morris names, becoming known just as Minis, and being sold in exactly the same form through both Austin and Morris dealerships. The dealer network was in any case quickly being rationalised and slimmed down as well. Another consideration was to make the Mini look more stylish and up-to-date, the result being the Roy Haynes-designed Mini Clubman with its longer and blunter front end, launched in October 1969 as part of the much-revised ADO 20 Mini range, which marked the end of the original 998cc Mini Cooper.

Available only with the 998cc engine in its basic single-carburettor 38bhp form, the Mini Clubman may have been considered by BLMC as a satisfactory 'replacement' for the various other mid-range Minis, such

The inimitable Brockbank illustrated BMC's original 1961 press release for the Mini Cooper... 'it needs but one corner to discover that what may be safe at 60mph on one type of car can be embarrassing, if not hazardous, on another...'

From the rear, the Mark II models of 1967-69 were distinguished by a wider rear window, larger rear lights and revised badging, including 'Mk II' script and a small '1000' to the right of the number plate.

as the Cooper, the Elf and the Hornet. While it had neither the Cooper's performance nor the traditional luxury touches of the Riley or the Wolseley, it certainly sold well enough with over 500,000 Clubman saloons and estates being made until these cars were discontinued in 1980. In 1969, the Clubman seemed to be the coming thing, and the Mini Cooper was yesterday's news. Only the Mini Cooper S was permitted to survive for a short

time, as related in the next chapter. However, the Clubman was such an uncharismatic car, inspiring neither excitement nor desire. Even the much-touted 1275 GT version was quite tame compared with the Mini Cooper S of similar capacity that it allegedly replaced. Eventually, 20 years later, in what was effectively a new company with very much a new management, the lesson of history was learned, and the Mini Cooper was recalled to life...

THE MINI COOPER S (1963-71)

The Mini Cooper S began in 1963 – or, as Philip Larkin might have put it, 'between the end of the Chatterley ban and *The Beatles'* first LP'. At first the more powerful S model was developed mainly for competition use: in the two years since its introduction the Mini Cooper had proved itself a worthy contender on the race tracks as well as in rallies, but there was obviously a limit to what could be achieved on 55bhp.

A close look reveals the small extra 'S' badge above the Austin Cooper bonnet badge – the only external indication of the more powerful model.

The impetus behind the development of a more powerful car again came from John Cooper. For the 1962 season his T59 Formula Junior racing car had used an 1100cc version of the BMC A-series engine, substantially

Even Royalty took to the Mini. Princess Margaret and Lord Snowdon, accompanied by the inevitable detective, are about to enter their Mini Cooper S.

bored out but – unlike the 997cc or 998cc Mini Cooper production engines – retaining the standard 848cc Mini's stroke of 68.3mm. The bore was increased to 71.6mm, with the end cylinders moved slightly outwards in the block, and cylinders number 2 and number 3 moved closer together, being siamesed with the loss of the central water passage. This race engine had a capacity fractionally under the 1100cc limit. The cylinder head had larger valves and the engine was claimed to give 98bhp, with a rev limit of 7800rpm.

This was a little over the top for what had to be a reasonably tractable and reliable road car, and where allowance also had to be made for a maximum rebore size of 40 thou (1mm). So when Eddie Maher of the engine factory in Coventry set about making a production version of Cooper's Formula Junior engine, he reduced the bore to 70.64mm which, in conjunction with the 68.26mm stroke, gave a capacity of 1071cc.

This still left room for valves of the same size as used on the racing engine – inlet valves were of 1.41in (35.72mm) diameter, exhaust valves of 1.22in (30.96mm) – giving valve areas of respectively a third and a half bigger than on any other A-series engine. The valves were made of the nickel alloy Nimonic 80, with stellite tips welded on to the stems. The valve guides were from a copper-nickel alloy called Hidural 5. Double valve springs and special forged rocker arms were used. Where other

Minis and the normal Mini Cooper had nine-stud cylinder heads, the S cylinder head was secured by ten studs and one bolt, with small notches cut into the rocker cover at either end to accommodate the extra stud and bolt – a valuable recognition point for anyone examining a Cooper S engine today.

The block followed the lay-out of the FJ engine, with more widely spaced cylinder bores and the centre pair of cylinders siamesed. Another important distinction point of the S engine was that it had removable tappet chest covers at the back of the engine (the manifold side). The only compression ratio available was 9.0:1. There was a new crankshaft, made of EN40B high-tensile steel, and nitrided for increased surface hardness. There were stiffer con rods, with a horizontally split big-end. The big-end journals were increased in diameter from 1.75in to 2in, while the width of the centre main bearing was slightly reduced from 1.063in to 1in. Special Brico pistons were used, with increased diameter gudgeon pins pressed into the little ends of the con rods, unlike the clamped gudgeon pins of the 997cc engine or the fully-floating con rods with circlip location of the 998cc unit.

Another difference from the lesser Cooper engines was that there was duplex chain drive to a new camshaft, although the valve timing was the same as for the 997/998cc units. The SU HS2 carburettors were also of the same size. The end result was that the 1071cc engine

A customised front end for another illustrious client: Alec Issigonis personally handed over this Austin Mini Cooper to Enzo Ferrari in 1964. Ferrari had a Mini. Issigonis did not have a Ferrari. Some customised cars were produced by BMC at Longbridge, notably this hatchback Mini Cooper S (below) built for Secretary of Transport Ernest Marples. The car still exists.

gave 70bhp (net) at 6200rpm, with maximum torque of 62lb ft (8.58mkg) at 4500rpm. Even more interesting was the beautifully flat torque curve: between 2500rpm and 5500rpm, torque did not drop below 60lb ft (8.3mkg). The safe rev limit was 7200rpm.

Surprisingly little was done to the rest of the car. An oil cooler was offered as an optional extra, subsequently becoming standard in order to conform to motor sport homologation requirements. The clutch had improved linings. An alternative final drive ratio of 3.444:1 was offered, and a closer-ratio gearbox could be fitted in conjunction with either final drive ratio. The front disc brakes were increased in diameter from 7in (178mm) to 7.5in (190.5mm), which enlarged the friction area, and the thickness of the brake discs was up from ¼in (6.35mm) to ⅜in (9.53mm) for greater heat dispersion. A Lockheed Hydrovac servo was fitted as standard equipment. Rear brakes were the same but the setting of the pressure-limiting valve was revised.

Standard tyre equipment was 5.00L–10 Dunlop C41 low-profile cross-plies, on the normal 3.50×10 Mini rim size, but – a first for any Mini – 145–10 Dunlop SP radial tyres were offered as an option, usually fitted to optional 4.50×10 rims which increased the track dimensions by 1in. On the S, the wheels – of either size – were drilled, perhaps for looks as much as for extra brake cooling. Very early S models with the wider wheels lacked hub caps but

these were quickly re-instated. The steering ratio was slightly higher.

A second fuel tank, installed symmetrically in the boot with its own filler on the right-hand side, was an optional extra and doubled capacity. This, like the oil cooler, eventually became standard equipment for homologation reasons. Externally, apart from the drilled wheels, there were only the additional 'S' letters of the front and rear badges to indicate that there was anything special about the new model, while the only change to the interior was that the 100mph (160kph) speedometer was replaced by one calibrated to 120mph (190kph).

The Mini Cooper S was launched in April 1963. It has often been described as a 'homologation special' as, at the time, international regulations called for 1000

examples of a production saloon car to be built in order to qualify for Group 1 homologation. Group 1 was then the most important class for rallying, and the Group 1 rules allowed hardly any modifications from standard catalogue specification – something which got BMC into trouble at the infamous 1966 Monte Carlo Rally (see pages 43-45)…

The development from Cooper to Cooper S followed exactly the same path that Ford took at the time, developing the Lotus-Cortina from the Cortina. The Lotus-engined Ford, in fact, had appeared only a few months earlier, in January 1963, so it is perhaps doubtful whether this potent but frail car influenced BMC's desire for a more powerful Mini Cooper version.

Whatever, the Cooper S was quickly homologated in Group 1 – this may have happened somewhat in advance of the production figure of 1000 being reached, although by the end of 1963 BMC had produced around 1700 of the cars, with Austin and Morris versions added together. The fact that, ostensibly, two different marque badges were involved obviously did not matter to the international motor sport authorities. It was also clear, right from the start, that the Mini Cooper S had enormous appeal, not just to the competition-minded fraternity but to a wider sector of the car-buying public.

Apart from the competition potential, what made the Cooper S such an attractive proposition was that, in 1963, no Q-car was more 'Q' – or, for that matter, more cute –

The 1275cc version was the quickest Cooper S. Its 75bhp engine gave 97mph and a 0-60mph time of 11sec – better than some two-seaters.

than the S. At £695, it was some £250 dearer than the basic Mini, apart from £125 more than a 997cc Mini Cooper, or £100 more than the Sprite-Midget twins. For about £700 you could buy an MG 1100 or a Riley One-Point-Five. A two-door Cortina GT, however, would set you back £749, and the Lotus-Cortina was an off-putting £1100. Of these potential rivals, it was only the Lotus-Cortina, with a top speed of 108mph (174kph), which would firmly close the door on a Cooper S. Yet the S had a top speed of 95mph (153kph) and would reach 60mph (96kph) in just under 13sec, offering performance which could worry all but the hardest-driven MGB.

Not only did the S have true sports car performance, but it offered all the proven advantages of Mini motoring: agile handling, a high degree of manoeuvrability, modest fuel consumption at anything up to 40mpg (7 litres per 100km) – if driven with decorum! – and a roomy interior. The few disadvantages to the S were common to all Minis: the unusual driving position, the uncomfortable seats and the uncompromising ride.

The model's greatest asset was the stunning performance, from a car which to most casual observers looked just like any other ordinary Mini. The unobtrusiveness of the Cooper S came to be appreciated

Under the bonnet of a 1275cc Cooper S model, with the brake servo as the most obvious clue to the nature of the car.

not least by those Police forces, notably Liverpool, which adopted the car for high-speed patrol use on the new motorways. As a further bit of camouflage, Police cars were usually painted plain white all over instead of being finished in typical two-tone Mini Cooper colours.

The changes implemented on the basic 997cc and later 998cc Cooper models were also introduced on the S, so there is little point here in repeating the information found in the previous chapter – except to stress that such specific engine-related changes as the introduction of the diaphragm spring clutch and the positive crankcase ventilation system also occurred on the 1071cc engine, at the same times as on the 998cc unit. However, in March 1964, after the 1071cc model had been in production for about a year, BMC launched two further versions of the Cooper S, with alternative capacities of 970cc and 1275cc respectively. The reason for this was to keep the car competitive in saloon car racing, where the 1000cc class was important on the international scene, and in rallying, where the small-car 1300cc class could be exploited.

Both of the new engine variations shared the 1071cc engine's bore of 70.64mm. The 970cc model had a very short stroke of only 61.91mm, and required a cylinder block, crankshaft, con rods, pistons and other parts which were unique to this engine size. The 1275cc version had a stroke of 81.33mm, which needed a taller block and a longer-throw crankshaft, although other parts were shared with the 1071cc engine. The cylinder head and the

camshaft were the same for all three sizes of the Cooper S engine. The 970cc had flat-top pistons and a compression ratio of 10.0:1, whereas the 1275cc had a slightly lower compression ratio of 9.75:1. The different engine number prefixes for the various Cooper S engines relate to the compression ratios: the 1071cc engine is 9F-SA-H (H for 9:1 compression), the 970cc engine is 9F-SA-X (X for 10:1 compression) and the 1275cc engine is 9F-SA-Y (Y for 9.75:1 compression).

The smaller engine developed 65bhp at 6500rpm and thanks to its short stroke was generally much happier to rev, although torque was only 55lb ft (7.6mkg) at 3500rpm. By contrast, the 1275cc engine gave its 75bhp at 5800rpm, with no less than 80lb ft (11.06mkg) of torque available at 3000rpm. Truly a case of different horses for different courses. On the 1275cc model, the higher final drive ratio of 3.444:1 was standard, but both the new variations were offered with a choice of alternative ratios.

The 970cc S was simply a homologation special, produced for less than one year. While BMC was required to produce 1000 to achieve Group 1 homologation, subsequent research shows that actual production is unlikely to have been more than 963 cars, split almost equally between Austin and Morris, and also split between rubber cone 'dry' cars and Hydrolastic 'wet' cars. Its price at launch was £671 although this was later increased to £693. Only a relatively small number of cars are likely to have been bought by owners who intended simply to go racing with them. It was a perfectly good road car, particularly exhilarating with its high-revving engine if obviously not as flexible as the other Mini Cooper models. It was so unusual – and perhaps deemed so specialised – that no full road test appears ever to have been carried out, but its top speed is estimated at around 92mph (148kph). It was available also with left-hand drive and 170-odd cars were exported. Nowadays, rarity makes it much sought-after.

By contrast, the 1275cc model was destined to become the most important of the Mini Cooper S models, while its engine size, of course, lives on to the present day, now as the only surviving variant of the A-series engine. The importance of the new model was underlined by the fact that the 1071cc model was discontinued in August 1964 – so all 1071cc cars therefore have the rubber cone suspension. The 1275cc model recorded a worthwhile improvement on the performance of the 1071cc car. Top speed was 97mph (156kph) – frustratingly no Mini Cooper in unmodified form would ever quite reach the 100mph mark! – and the 0-60mph (0-96kph) time was down to a highly respectable 11sec. In third gear, 30-50mph (48-80kph) went by in just 5sec, while *Motor* magazine recorded a remarkable 7.8sec for 10-30mph (16-48kph) in *top* gear – demonstrating the engine's remarkable flexibility.

In common with other early 1275cc cars, however, the test car used by *Motor* was found to be rather rough and noisy compared with other Mini Coopers. The magazine also got no more than 75 miles to a pint of oil; overall fuel consumption was around the 30mpg mark (9.5 litres per 100km). The car was summed up as 'enormous fun to drive and just about the most practical toy that £750 will buy'. To be precise, the exact price was £756, while at the time the 1071cc model cost £695 and the 998cc version £568. Prices were increased, however, in October 1964, the 998cc model going up to £590 and the 1275cc to £778. Compared with the 1275cc S, the Ford Cortina GT cost £749: it was both slower and thirstier, and whoever needed a boot of that size anyway? Going to the other extreme, the performance of the Cooper S 1275 was closely comparable with that of the MGB, but this open two-seater cost £835 and offered neither the practicality of the Cooper (the MGB GT was yet to come) nor, arguably, the same fun factor.

After the 1071cc and 970cc models had been discontinued, the 1275cc went ahead on its own. Most changes over the following years were again the same as those implemented on the 998cc model, thus only the

Although photographed in the Export Department at Cowley, this extraordinarily decorated Mini Cooper S was in fact customised by Radford and reputedly destined for a VIP customer somewhere abroad. The interior has a wealth of luxury features, including electric windows – the only jarring note is struck by Dymo labels on the additional switch panel!

early 1275 cars had the rubber suspension, changed in the autumn of 1964 for Hydrolastic. Some engine changes, however, were unique to the S model. Thus in January 1966 an improved camshaft was fitted, later that year the inboard rubber drive couplings on the drive shafts were replaced by solid universal joints, and in September 1966 a new cross-drilled crankshaft was introduced. At some stage, probably in January 1966, the additional right-hand fuel tank and an uprated 13-row oil cooler became standard on the S model. Both of these additions were due to homologation requirements, as these parts could only be used in competition if they were demonstrably standard on production cars.

This Mini Cooper S Mark II interior is from a very early car of this type, unusually not with the all-black trim that soon became standard.

The optional reclining seats did something to improve the famously awkward driving position of the Mini. Enlarged tail lamp units are an instant Mark II identifying feature. The boot lid badge used the words 'Mini Cooper S Mk II' and was supplemented by a small '1275' badge to the right of the number plate.

Another effect of homologation was that production of the S was drastically stepped up in 1965 when the rules for Group 1 cars were changed and 5000 cars had to be produced over a 12-month period. To quote rally historian Graham Robson, 'this was the moment when wholesale cheating by manufacturers appeared to intensify'. BMC at least came very close to meeting the new requirement – the best possible production figure that has been established suggests that precisely 4987 1275cc cars were made in 1965, to which one might with a bit of goodwill add the rump of 970cc production of 118 cars. The tempo was kept up with 4103 cars made in 1966 but then it slowed down again.

The desired homologation was duly granted but a side effect was that many Mini Cooper S models sat in dealer showrooms for a long time. Some cars in the home market were only sold when they were a year or more old – so much for the desirability factor of the car! One also wonders what the oversupply situation did to second-hand values at the time…

The Mini Cooper S Mark II.................

In 1967 the Mini Cooper S went into Mark II form, with exactly the same changes as detailed in the previous chapter for the Mini Cooper. It deserves to be mentioned

31

Police Mini Coopers were often all-white, although this ex-Liverpool Police car has the black roof. It is fitted with the correct roof sign and other Police equipment. The original Liverpool Police Mini Cooper S Mark IIs are seen (facing page) in their all-white livery.

Three very famous Mini Coopers – the stars of 'The Italian Job'.

that while the bonnet badge of the Mini Cooper S Mark II still stated the 'Austin' or 'Morris' name, the boot lid badge – shared by both marques – for the first time identified the car as a 'Mini Cooper' ('S Mark II'). In addition, a small '1275' badge appeared to the right of the number plate – the ordinary Mini Cooper Mark II had a similar '1000' in this position.

For quite some time the Mini Cooper S had been the only Mini version to be sold in the USA, but at the end of 1967 it was withdrawn from this market because the Mini could not be made compatible with the new US safety standards which came into force from 1 January 1968. One fundamental reason was that its wheelbase was shorter than the minimum prescribed by the new legislation. The Mini was still accepted in Canada, however, and indeed continued to sell there for another ten years.

The all-synchromesh gearbox arrived on the S model in 1968 at the same time as on the 998cc model, with the engine number prefix being altered form 9F-SA-Y to 9F-XE-Y. On the other hand, the 1969 changes to the

engine number prefix system were not implemented on the S before the advent of the Mark III model in 1970 (see page 35). One late change, in November 1969, to affect only the Cooper S engine was that the bronze valve guides were replaced by steel, while the valve stems were chromed. Some late Mark II engines may have had the cheaper tuftrided crankshaft found on the Mark III, and it is also thought that at some stage during Mark II production an improved cylinder head, casting number 12G 940, was introduced – this was less prone to cracking between the inlet and exhaust valve seats.

Production of the Mark II S lasted a little longer than of the 998cc model, and the last cars were only built in February 1970. Perhaps because of this, some of the last cars are also believed to have been finished in single-tone colours from the range found on the revised Minis. The revised Mini range, with the project code ADO 20, had gone into production in the autumn of 1969 and was thus well-established by the time the final Mini Cooper S Mark II came off the line.

The beige-and-white colour scheme was one of the less popular choices for the Mark II, but this is a superb example of this later Mini Cooper S model. Its 1275cc engine is presented to concours standard: just visible are the extra cylinder head stud (by the heater water valve on the left) and the extra bolt (by the thermostat housing on the right), indicating that this is an S engine. Boot view shows extra right-hand fuel tank and narrower boot board.

ODL 975H

Single-colour schemes came in with the Mark III, which on the whole looked just like other short-nose Minis of the 1970-71 period – excepting the boot badge and the wheels, larger than standard here. The 12H-type engine of the Mark III was painted all black, and the brake servo was of a different type compared with earlier models.

The Mini Cooper S Mark III...............

Almost as an afterthought, a Mini Cooper S Mark III went into production in March 1970. It lasted only 15 months and only around 1570 cars were made at Longbridge, although substantial numbers of Coopers were still being produced in CKD form for assembly abroad.

The Mark III version had an in house competitor in the shape of the new Mini 1275 GT, sharing the Clubman bodyshell and fitted with a 59bhp version of the 1275cc engine. This was naturally slower than the Mini Cooper, being flat out at 90mph (145kph), but was destined to become a much bigger seller – a total of 110,000 1275 GTs were made until 1980.

Compared with previous models, the Mini Cooper S Mark III was in many ways a radical alteration. The new

Mark III Minis had concealed door hinges and winding windows, but only the pierced wheels and right-hand fuel filler tell us that this is a Cooper S version. The interior is very much like other Minis of the period, only the 130mph speedometer giving the game away.

ADO 20 bodyshell was substantially changed, inside and out. Its most obvious features were internal door hinges, and winding instead of sliding windows. Such previously distinguishing features as the grille, bonnet badge and colour schemes were now shared with all other 'short-nosed' Minis; only the boot lid badge proclaimed the car to be a Mini Cooper S. The interior trim was also shared with other Minis and was very similar to the Mark II model, the major difference being that there were no longer any door bins, because of the winding windows, but simple door trim panels instead.

In mechanical terms there were fewer changes. The engine was given a new prefix code starting with 12H, and the engines were typically painted black rather than the traditional BMC engine green. The crankshaft was now tuftrided – a cheaper process – rather than nitrided. During the Mark III production run the original forged valve rockers were also replaced by cheaper pressed steel rockers. Hydrolastic suspension was still used on the Mark III although other short-nosed Minis in the ADO 20 range had gone back to the solid rubber cone suspension; opinions still differ as to whether a few of the last Mark

Of the 'wannabe' Cooper replacements, the 1275GT was the most potent but even this was a disappointment compared with the 1275cc S. This 1974 model features the rarely-seen optional Denovo tyres.

IIIs originally had the rubber suspension. The brake servo was slightly bigger, and the electrical system was now of the negative earth type, reflecting the fact that alternators were beginning to oust dynamos in production (the Mark III could be fitted with either).

Not many important changes were made to the Mark III during its short production life, but in October 1970 an ignition shield was fitted, while in January 1971 home market cars were fitted with a steering lock (previously often found on export models) and seat belts became factory-fitted rather than dealer-fitted. Also around this time, the original toggle-type switches for lights and wipers were replaced by flat rocker switches. The Mark III was only ever available in single-tone colours, shared with other Minis, but at least a bit of colour returned to the interiors, as most paint colours were offered with a choice of two or more different interior trim colours.

In terms of performance there was nothing to choose between the Mini Cooper S Mark III and its predecessors. The price of the car was £1008, compared with £894 for the 1275 GT.

It is now difficult to determine whether public interest in the Mini Cooper had totally evaporated, or whether BLMC deliberately under-promoted and under-supplied the car. Whatever, it is clear that Donald Stokes wanted to terminate the old royalty agreement with John Cooper at the end of the ten years originally stipulated. Stokes simply resented spending money when it seemed unnecessary – he also cancelled the similar agreement with Donald Healey regarding the Austin-Healey marque – and it is thought that he also disliked having effectively to give credit to somebody outside his company for the success of the cars in question. John Cooper was given notice that the agreement would not be renewed, and in June 1971 the last Mini Cooper S Mark III came off the production line. As related in a subsequent chapter (see pages 53-59), production in Spain and Italy continued, as their respective agreements with Cooper also had a ten-year run but had come into force much later.

After ten years in production, more than 100,000 Mini Coopers had been built and the cars had scored some of the most outstanding British successes in the world of international motor sport – yet there seems to have been very little reaction to the news that the car was going out of production. Greater furore attended the demise of such brands as Riley and Austin-Healey – both of them also early victims of the Stokes-inspired purge of British Leyland. Naturally, with the effective closure of the BMC Competitions Department the Mini Cooper was not quite so much in the public eye (and the car was no longer seriously competitive in rallying anyway) and British motor sports enthusiasts were busy cheering a new champion, the Ford Escort.

As so often happens with recently discontinued cars, for some years the Mini Cooper remained neglected and somewhat overlooked. By contrast, however, the Mini itself had some of its best years in terms of production in the early 1970s. Only in the 1980s did the original Mini Cooper acquire status as a true classic car, and since then world-wide interest in these cars has continued to increase. The car that was a legend in its own lifetime has become a legend once again.

MINI COOPERS IN COMPETITION

The legend of the Mini Cooper was largely built on its competition successes. As mentioned at the start of this book, it was never the intention or desire of Alec Issigonis that his masterpiece should be used for serious motor sport, and it is to others, chief among them John Cooper, but also to Stuart Turner and his team at BMC's Competitions Department, that we owe the inspiration and dedication that were needed to turn this unassuming baby car into one of the most popular British competition cars ever.

There are, in effect, two stories to be told here. The better-known aspect of the Mini's competition career is as a rally car, mostly in the hands of the works team, but the car also had a respectable career on the racing circuits. And while it was always the Mini Cooper that gathered most of the laurels, the competition career of the Mini was well under way before the Cooper versions appeared.

Paddy Hopkirk's victory in the 1964 Monte Carlo Rally (top) remains a cherished memory, the most famous of all the Mini Cooper successes. In the same event Timo Makinen (above) finished fourth in this sister car.

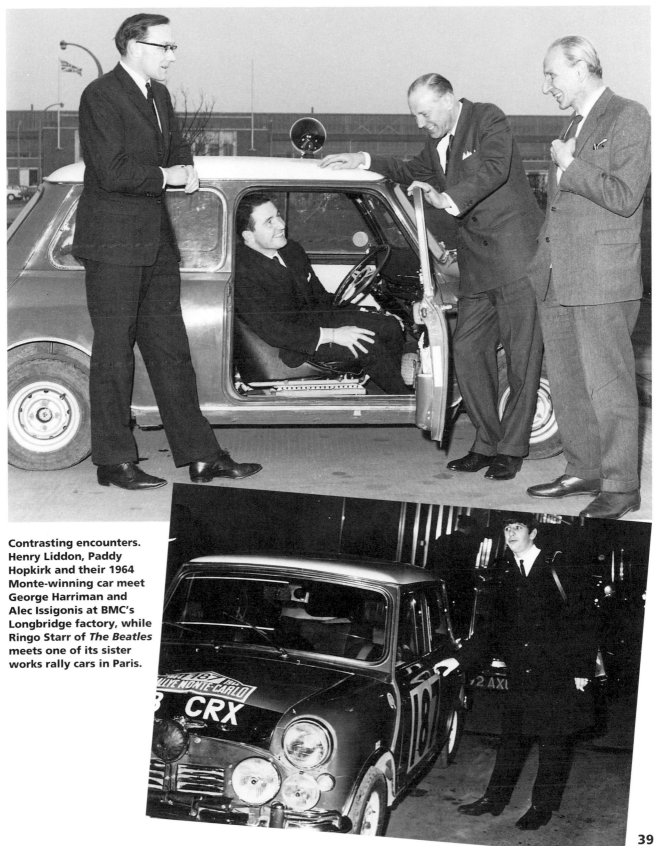

Contrasting encounters. Henry Liddon, Paddy Hopkirk and their 1964 Monte-winning car meet George Harriman and Alec Issigonis at BMC's Longbridge factory, while Ringo Starr of *The Beatles* meets one of its sister works rally cars in Paris.

Pre-Cooper BMC works rally cars: none of the three cars entered for the 1961 Monte finished the event.

Rauno Aaltonen drove 277 EBL, the first 1071cc S model to be used by the BMC team, to victory on its debut outing in the 1963 Alpine Rally.

Pauline Mayman (on the left) and Val Domleo with their 970cc Mini Cooper S on the 1964 Alpine Rally (at times the same car also ran with a 1275cc engine). Not much in the way of crowd control (below) in the 1965 Czech Rally: these are the winners, Aaltonen and Ambrose.

Great activity in the famous BMC Competitions Department workshop at Abingdon, a few days before the 1965 **RAC Rally, with Tony Fall's entry in the foreground. Wonder what happened to all the rally plates on the far wall?**

Mini Coopers in rallying ....

BMC in the mid-1950s decided to re-establish a Competitions Department (after a virtual absence from the sport since MG pulled out in 1935) because the company's management, after much lobbying from interested parties, became convinced that success in motor sport would lead to good publicity and, in turn, increased sales – the well-known 'win on Sunday, sell on Monday' theory.

The company's efforts, originally managed by Marcus Chambers, got off to a somewhat shaky start, and it was only after much experimenting with different BMC products in a variety of events that the department hit its first jackpot with the Austin-Healey 3000. Just as this car was getting into its stride, an entirely new possibility was opened up when the Mini became available. It is

interesting to note that although BMC's Competitions Department had been started up at the beginning of 1955, the first overall win for one of its entries came in 1959 – and then with a Mini, in the Mini Miglia rally, as related earlier (see page 11).

Over the next couple of years BMC made increasing use of Minis. As early as the 1960 Monte Carlo Rally, the company entered six Minis – three Austins, three Morrises – but none finished better than 23rd overall. The original 848cc cars were capable of the occasional class win, such as in the 1960 Alpine and 1961 Tulip rallies, while the best overall result was sixth in the 1960 RAC Rally – but nothing better was achieved. Then in 1961 the Mini Cooper came along and was quickly seized on by the Competitions Department. Almost at the same time, Marcus Chambers left the department, to be replaced by Stuart Turner, under whose management for the next six years BMC and the Mini would reap their greatest rewards.

The star driver of the 1962 season was undoubtedly Pat Moss, driving either an Austin-Healey 3000 or a Mini Cooper. She achieved the first overall victory for the Mini Cooper in the 1962 Tulip Rally, and went on

41

The only win for the Mini Cooper in the RAC Rally came in 1965, and Rauno Aaltonen was the driver. Here he is seen at Oulton Park race circuit and at a symbolic night-time moment in the snow. After stopping to help snow-bound team-mates Makinen and Easter in the Healey, which went on to finish second, Aaltonen rejoins navigator Ambrose waiting patiently in the Cooper S.

On a hiding to nothing. At the end of the 1966 Monte Carlo Rally Timo Makinen was in first place, only to be disqualified for a trivial lighting infringement. The gesture at post-rally scrutineering is worth a thousand words…

Aaltonen negotiates a tricky hairpin bend on his way to victory in the 1967 Monte – a graffiti artist has done his bit to egg on the works Minis.

to become European Ladies' Rally Champion that year. Also during 1962, BMC signed up three drivers who, more than anybody else, would become identified with the Mini and its successes – the Irishman Paddy Hopkirk, and the two famous 'flying Finns', Rauno Aaltonen and Timo Makinen. The three came together for the first time in the 1962 RAC Rally, Aaltonen and Makinen (his first drive for BMC) already in Mini Coopers – they came fifth and seventh overall – while Hopkirk, who came second, was still in an Austin-Healey.

They were well on their way. The 1963 season opened with Aaltonen taking third overall in a Mini Cooper in the Monte Carlo Rally, Hopkirk following him home in sixth place in a similar car. Then the Mini Cooper S became available and it fell to Aaltonen to give the new model its first outing in the 1963 Alpine Rally – and he won outright. The rest of the season was perhaps an anticlimax, but Hopkirk also made his mark by taking third place in the Tour de France – in the car registered 33 EJB, soon to become even more famous – and coming fourth in the RAC Rally.

The number of Minis appearing in major rallying events had steadily increased ever since 1960. In the 1964 Monte Carlo Rally there were no fewer than 36 assorted Mini Coopers, mostly S models: in addition to the six works cars, there were 30 private entrants, mostly British but with a sprinkling from other countries. It was Hopkirk, with co-driver Henry Liddon, who came home

the winner, starting form Minsk in Russia in the Tour de France car 33 EJB, but Makinen and Aaltonen were not far behind, in fourth and seventh places respectively.

In April it was Makinen's turn to taste victory, in the Tulip Rally with the first entry for the new 1275cc S model. In the Alpine Rally two months later, Aaltonen won his class and one of the much-coveted *Coupe des Alpes* awards. In the same event there was a rare entry for the 970cc model, as Pauline Mayman and Val Domleo won their class and took the ladies' cup. They were to repeat the class win in the same car in the Tour de France later in the year.

From now on the 1275cc model would dominate and 1965 brought further successes, starting with victory for Makinen and Paul Easter in the Monte Carlo Rally. Hopkirk won the Circuit of Ireland but it was really Aaltonen's year: having retired in the Monte, he was the winner of the Geneva Rally, the Rally Vltava in Czechoslovakia, the Polish Rally, the Munich-Vienna-Budapest Rally and, most importantly, at the end of the season he scored the only victory for the works Minis in Britain's premier rally, the RAC. Rauno and the Mini Cooper S were the European Rally Champions of 1965. The Monte winner, Makinen, put up a spirited drive in the RAC and finished second, but earlier in the year had won the Thousand Lakes Rally in his native Finland.

Naturally, hopes were high for the 1966 season. Makinen, Aaltonen and Hopkirk set out on the Monte

Typical interior of a works rally car, in this case one of the Mark II cars prepared for the 1968 season. Most surprising bit of equipment – the cigar lighter in front of the passenger.

Carlo in three brand-new cars and finished a remarkable first, second and third overall – only to find themselves at the centre of a furious row. They, and other British works entries, were disqualified, apparently to allow a French car – Pauli Toivonen's Citroën DS19 – to win Europe's most prestigious event. The French rally organisers appeared to doubt that the Mini Cooper S cars really were to standard specification, or that BMC had really made the required 5000 in the previous 12-month period. Some exceedingly detailed post-rally scrutineering did prove that the lighting system on the BMC Minis was not operated as per the standard production car, so there was undoubtedly an infringement of the technical regulations, however slight and inconsequential. BMC accepted this as the final verdict, with as much good grace as they could muster at the time. Undoubtedly the whole sorry episode gave the company, its cars and its drivers far more publicity exposure than would have been the case if they had won without any protest, especially in the British press where feelings ran predictably high.

During the remainder of the 1966 season, a more recent recruit to the BMC team, Tony Fall, came to the fore with overall wins in the Circuit of Ireland, as well as the Scottish and Polish rallies. Aaltonen took the honours in the Tulip Rally and the Czech Rally Vltava, Hopkirk won the Austrian Alpine Rally, while Makinen was victorious in the Thousand Lakes and the Munich-Vienna-

Budapest. The highest-placed works Mini in the RAC was that of the 'new boys', the Swedes Harry Kallstrom and co-driver Haakansson, who finished second.

The next year, 1967, was to be the last great year for the Mini in rallying. After the set-back in the previous year, no doubt the most cherished victory was in the Monte Carlo Rally for Aaltonen and Liddon, who were followed home by Hopkirk in sixth place. Otherwise it was Hopkirk's year, with a repeat win in the Circuit of Ireland, and other victories in the Acropolis and Alpine rallies. Other team members also had their moments – Fall came first in the Geneva Rally and Makinen won the Thousand Lakes Rally yet again to register a remarkable hat-trick on this Finnish event.

A major effort was prepared for the RAC Rally. After the protest-ridden 1966 season, rally regulations were being relaxed to allow rather more radical modifications from standard specification, and a fuel-injected Mini Cooper S was built for Timo Makinen to take on the RAC – which was then cancelled at short notice owing to the outbreak in Britain of foot-and-mouth disease.

During 1967, Stuart Turner had retired as BMC's competitions manager, and had been replaced by Peter Browning. The change in fortunes for BMC's Competitions Department in 1968 and later, however, had nothing to do with the change in management – Browning was just as experienced and capable as his predecessor – but was caused by other factors. The

Tony Fall in the forest on the 1966 RAC Rally on his way to fifth place. The engine bay is from another of the 1966 works cars, in this case GRX 5D. Apart from extra driving lights, note the alternator, the air horns and the small separate air cleaners.

BMC came back to Monte Carlo with a vengeance in 1967. Aaltonen won, and Hopkirk (above) followed him in sixth place. A new recruit to the BMC team was Finnish driver Simo Lampinen (right), who finished 15th.

ill-starred merger of BMC with Leyland in early 1968 would lead to the original Competitions Department being virtually disbanded in 1970, and a change of emphasis in the international rally regulations virtually put the Cooper S out of contention – the new star in rallying was the Porsche 911.

So 1968 became the last season for a major rallying programme. Aaltonen's third place in the Monte, with Fall and Hopkirk coming fourth and fifth, was impressive bearing in mind that Porsche 911s finished one-two. There were in fact no overall wins for the Mini Coopers in 1968, the best of the other results being third overall in the Tulip Rally (Belgian driver Julien Vernaeve), second in the Scottish Rally (the Swede Lars-Ingvar Ytterbring) and second in the Portuguese TAP Rally (Paddy Hopkirk's swansong).

For 1969, the BLMC Competitions Department turned briefly to rallycross, a sport whose main advantage

was that the events were televised in Britain, and also to a programme of racing Mini Coopers, the first time that works Minis – as opposed to private ones with some works support – had been raced. Into 1970, the competition career of the Mini Cooper largely came to an end – works driver Brian Culcheth had a couple of entries in Australian rallies, and eight privately entered Mini Coopers still contested the Monte, but that was really it.

Mini Coopers in racing ....

We must go all the way back to 1961 to look at the career of the Mini Cooper in saloon car racing. Minis had been entered in racing ever since 1959, when, for instance, Daniel Richmond's first Downton Mini appeared on the circuits, but the first outstanding successes for the original cars with their 848cc engines

Intense duelling among the Mini drivers enlivened this 1966 race at Crystal Palace. The occasion was the London Trophy meeting on Whit Monday, Gordon Spice being pressured by Tony Lanfranchi and another driver.

came in 1961, when Sir John Whitmore won the British Saloon Car Championship. While the races in this championship were contested by cars of widely differing size and engine capacity, points were awarded in each of four classes which gave the smaller-engined cars a fairer chance against large-capacity machines. Thus, while the Minis were rarely in the running for overall victory, consistent results in class could lead to the championship being won by a Mini.

For the 1962 season, John Cooper set up his saloon car racing team with the new Mini Coopers, supported by BMC, and with Whitmore and John Love as the drivers. Love won the championship, giving the Mini two in a row. This success attracted the interest of other racing teams, and for 1963 Ralph Broad of Broadspeed set up a Mini team to contest the championship, with drivers including John Fitzpatrick, John Handley, Jeff May and Peter Tempest – although this was initially an entirely private effort and was not supported by BMC. The Cooper team continued to enjoy BMC support and Whitmore was still its principal driver, although Paddy Hopkirk occasionally came along as well.

Sir John mostly drove the new Mini Cooper S during the 1963 season and finished up with second place in the championship, and a 1300cc class win. The year's overall championship winner was Jack Sears who contested some of the races in the mighty Ford Galaxie, a total contrast to the Mini Cooper but a car that did much to enliven the races it took part in! The Mini Coopers now also appeared in the European Touring Car Championship,

British Grand Prix meeting at Brands Hatch in 1966. The Cooper versus Anglia battle unfolds, with a Triumph 2000, a couple of Imps, a Lotus-Cortina, and a big bad black Mustang rumbling up from behind. Crystal Palace (right), 1966: John Rhodes gets the inside rear wheel off the ground. The 1968 Cooper team cars featured this more prominent livery (below right) and the first sponsors' stickers were appearing. Rhodes, with Steve Neal tucked in behind, burns rubber in his time-honoured style.

John Cooper checking over his team's tyres in 1969, with the newly-liveried yellow Britax-Cooper-Downton cars. British Leyland for the first time had its own entries in saloon car racing in 1969 (below), with drivers John Rhodes and John Handley, but this effort brought little success. Alec Poole, the private Equipe Arden driver (below right), took the 1969 British saloon car title with this 970cc Cooper S.

Dutchman Rob Slotemaker winning the 1300cc class in a Downton-prepared Cooper S, while John Aley was second in the 1000cc class in his 997cc Cooper.

The British and European championships were both contested by the Cooper team in 1964, with Ken Tyrrell looking after the European side of things on Cooper's behalf. Although Jim Clark in the Lotus-Cortina won the British championship, John Fitzpatrick of the Cooper team was second and won the 1300cc class. In Europe, Warwick Banks in his Tyrrell-Cooper 970cc Cooper S took the overall championship. This was a highly satisfactory result also to BMC, as Cooper's backers, although for the 1965 season BMC decided that the Cooper team should concentrate on the British championship, while the Broadspeed team, now with BMC backing, should contest the European championship. The results were better for the Cooper

team at home, with Banks in a 970cc car coming second in the British championship and winning the 1000cc class, while team-mate John Rhodes in a 1275cc car won the 1300cc class and came third overall. Banks and Rhodes, incidentally, took in the Spa 24-hour race during this season.

The Broadspeed contract was not renewed for 1966. Instead Ralph Broad took his team into the Ford camp, and his driver, John Fitzpatrick, was that year's British champion in a Ford Anglia fitted with a Formula 3 engine – the British championship was now run to Group 5 regulations which permitted a degree of latitude in such matters. The Cooper team was still in the running, with Rhodes coming second in the championship, a result that he would repeat in 1967. In 1968, BMC again decided to support two teams. At home, the Cooper team continued, still with Rhodes as

At Silverstone in 1969, one of the BL works cars followed by a Cooper team car – neither team was successful in that year's championship.

the principal driver, and he finished equal third in what was now the RAC Saloon Car Championship. In Europe, BMC supported the British Vita team. No overall winner of the European championship was declared but moral victory belonged to British Vita driver John Handley, who scored the highest number of points and won the 1000cc class, also called Division 1.

With the BMC works rally team on the wane, the company decided to stop supporting external racing teams and instead launched its own entries in the British championship in 1969. Rhodes and Handley were the drivers but they got off to a less than auspicious start by both crashing their brand-new cars in the first race of the season. In consequence some rather elderly rally cars were wheeled out of retirement to allow the programme to continue…

It is a moot point how competitive the Mini Coopers were by this stage, and neither Rhodes nor Handley could usually do much better than second or third in class. Only in the very last race of the year, at the Salzburgring in Austria in October, did Rhodes and Handley finish first and second overall respectively – this was also the last race of all for the works Mini Coopers.

In 1969 BLMC could, however, bask in the reflected glory of the private team Equipe Arden, whose driver Alec Poole won the British championship in his 970cc Mini Cooper S, proving once again that a consistent record in a small-capacity car was just as likely, if not more likely, to bring success in the championship overall than the occasional outright win in individual races. And what of the original Cooper team? It ran Downton-prepared cars in 1969, with sponsorship from Britax, and with Gordon Spice and Steve Neal as the drivers. Despite the occasional outright win, they stood no chance against the Ford Escorts in the 1300cc class.

This was the last year for the Cooper team, and the Mini Coopers now faded from the racing scene as they were fading from the world of rallying. But there was still some glory to come for the Mini: in 1978 and again in 1979, Richard Longman won the British Saloon Car Championship with his Mini 1275 GT.

Of the other events contested by the Mini Cooper throughout its career, two one-offs deserve a mention. BMC had long contested the 12-hour sports car race at Sebring in the USA, for the benefit of US enthusiasts for MG and Austin-Healey, but in 1967 decided also to enter the supporting 3-hour saloon car race with Paddy Hopkirk and John Rhodes driving a Mini Cooper S. They were rewarded with a first in class. In August of the same year, the works team entered two 970cc cars in that 84-hour torture, the Marathon de la Route held at the Nürburgring. The car driven by Alec Poole, Roger Enever and Clive Baker retired after an accident, but Tony Fall, Julien Vernaeve and Andrew Hedges finished second – all the more creditable a performance when one bears in mind that the winner was a Porsche 911.

MINI COOPERS WORLD-WIDE

The sun sets over the Empire: atmospheric shot of an Australian Mini Cooper S. Nearly 7500 of these cars were made between 1965-71.

When, after 1945, the British motor industry began to take the export market seriously, spurred on by government policies and directives, British cars began to find their way into some quite surprising markets. The original Empire or Commonwealth markets still remained important, but much effort was put into cultivating the North American markets, as well as many different European countries.

Australian Mini Coopers...................

One of the difficulties encountered was that some countries erected tariff barriers, usually in an effort to encourage their indigenous motor industry. Thus in 1952 Australia, one of the most important outlets for British

cars in the early post-war period, but where the locally-made Holden car was rapidly gaining in popularity, began to impose a much higher rate of duty on fully-assembled cars. To remain competitive in this market, the major British car makers had no alternative but to set up local manufacturing operations, with an increasing percentage of locally-sourced parts.

BMC accordingly set up an Australian company with a factory in Sydney, turning out a variety of cars, some simply assembled from CKD (Completely Knocked Down) kits sent out from Britain. Gradually other models were introduced with a higher Australian content, sometimes of unique design – such as the Austin Lancer and Morris Major of 1958, both based on the Wolseley 1500 design. By the early 1960s, the most popular small car in the Australian market was the locally-made Volkswagen Beetle, so BMC decided to bring the Mini into production in Australia. The first Australian-assembled Mini-Minors – the model was originally known there as the Morris 850 – appeared in March 1961, and production quickly built up to 16,000 cars per year (for comparison, the best year for the VW Beetle in Australia was 1964 with more than 25,000 cars built).

The Mini Cooper followed, going into production in Australia in late 1962, priced at £A950; the Morris 850 then cost £A740. The Australian Mini Coopers were sent out as partial CKD kits from Longbridge and were each assigned a chassis number in the normal series for Longbridge-built Minis, although when they were assembled in the Sydney factory, each was given a special Australian chassis number, with a prefix code beginning with the letter Y which in BMC terminology indicated Australian manufacture. The 997cc and later 998cc Australian Mini Coopers were fitted with the low-compression (8.3:1) engines and power output was quoted as 52bhp at 6000rpm – but the road test in *Modern Motor* recorded a top speed of 86.7mph (139.5kph), nearly as good as the slightly more powerful British car. Incidentally, the road tester managed to discuss the *rear*-axle ratio of the car!

At this time, differences between British and Australian Minis were comparatively slight and mainly confined to such parts as were locally sourced – thus the Australian Mini Cooper had single-colour interior trim, different seat patterns, and flecked rather than monotone carpet material. In addition to a range of two-tone exterior colour schemes, all-black was listed as a standard colour. The 998cc model superseded the 997cc model in early 1964, but in the autumn of that year shipments of CKD kits to Australia ceased, after an estimated total of about 4000 cars. All of the Australian-assembled cars were badged Morris, and all had rubber cone suspension. The Mini Cooper was replaced by a new de-luxe version of the Morris Mini-Minor which had similar trim and the remote control gearchange, and a single carburettor version of the 998cc engine.

However, in mid-1965 BMC Australia began assembly of the Mini Cooper S 1275cc. These cars were again shipped out from Longbridge in CKD form, complete with the normal 1275cc high-compression engine. They had Hydrolastic suspension, but one of the

BMC's incredible minis

now more incredible than ever

the world its proving ground

By 1967 the Australian Minis were 'more incredible than ever' –

and all shared the same Morris Cooper-style radiator grille.

modifications for the Australian version was to recess and box in the connecting pipes on the underside of the car. Another important difference was that the cars had winding door windows with quarterlights. Both these features suggest that BMC Australia was by now pressing some panels locally. The interior trim was similar to the previous Mini Coopers, while equipment included a laminated windscreen and seat belts.

Production of this Cooper S model continued until 1969, when it was replaced by a Mark II version, and around the same time Australian-assembled cars acquired the all-synchromesh gearbox. The Australian Mark II had an all-black interior and bolt-on wheel arch extensions but retained the Mark I-type radiator grille, rear window and rear lights. Also in 1969, BMC Australia introduced the Morris Mini K with a 1098cc engine and 80 per cent local content. This and the Mini Cooper continued in production until 1971, when all Australian Minis were given the Clubman-type bodyshell, and a 1275 GT version replaced the Mini Cooper. Almost 7500 Australian-made Cooper S cars were built.

The Mini Cooper S found favour also with the Sydney Police, here under the city's most famous landmark in the days before the opera house.

Innocenti in Italy.............................

Tariff barriers also explain BMC's efforts to assemble cars in a number of European countries. Before Britain joined the EEC in 1973, it was important to have a manufacturing base in at least one EEC country as member states charged very much lower tariffs on EEC-sourced cars. For instance, in 1967 a small British car imported into Italy attracted duty at the rate of 31.2 per cent, but the levy on French or German cars was only 9 per cent – and similar differences applied in other EEC countries. Spain still stood outside the European trading blocks and levied up to 70 per cent duty on all imports, to protect her own fledgling motor industry, mainly the Fiat-supported SEAT operation but also off-shoots of Renault, Citroën and Simca.

Italy and Spain both became targets for BMC. Italy was the most rapidly developing of the major European car markets, and Spain was potentially an equally important market for the future. Italy had the additional attraction that a manufacturing operation there could

supply other EEC countries at preferential rates of duty, as with Belgium where BMC also decided to set up local manufacture.

At the end of the 1950s Italy was just about to enter the era of mass motorisation. In the immediate post-war period, many requirements for personal transport had been met by the Vespa and Lambretta scooters, but their role was about to be usurped by Fiat's 'Nuova 500', launched in 1957. Both scooter manufacturers looked at getting into car manufacture; a Vespa car was subsequently made in France, while the makers of the Lambretta, the brothers Innocenti whose background was in metal pressings and press tools, decided to talk to BMC. In 1959 an agreement was concluded for Innocenti to manufacture the Austin A40 under licence, with a locally-made body and mechanical components shipped out from England. It was followed by the Innocenti Spyder (an Austin-Healey Sprite with a new body styled by Ghia), the Innocenti IM3 (based on the Morris 1100) and, in 1965, the first Innocenti Mini.

The Mini in its various forms soon became Innocenti's most important product. An estimated 400,000 Minis were built in Milan from 1965 to 1976, and the company's annual output reached over 60,000 cars in the early 1970s. Innocenti built the Mini Minor 850 saloon, the Mini Traveller which they called the Mini t, and the automatic saloon which became the Mini-Matic. Most of the production was sold in the Italian home market. Although Innocenti was very small beer compared with gargantuan Fiat and the Minis were more expensive than the small Fiats, they attracted a strong following and were frequently seen in Italy during their heyday.

Innocenti launched the first Mini Cooper in March 1966. Mechanical components came from Longbridge and Coventry, including Hydrolastic suspension and a 56bhp engine to a slightly different specification from the engine used in British-built cars. Many body panels were pressed by Innocenti, while trim, instruments, electrical equipment and many other parts were sourced in Italy, often to Innocenti's own unique specification. Identification points were a modified radiator grille, Innocenti badges and some unique colour schemes.

In 1968 an upgraded Mark I model featured a new dashboard moulding with five instruments (including a rev counter), new seats and a radiator grille similar to the UK-built Mini Cooper Mark II, while the proper Innocenti Mark II arrived later that year, now with a 60bhp engine thanks to a higher compression ratio of 9.5:1. The Mark II also had larger rear light units with

The early Innocenti Mini Coopers are now very rare. This is a Mark I version from the 1966-68 period.

Brochure images of the Innocenti Mini Cooper Mark III clearly show large headlamp bezels, front indicator repeaters, Rostyle-type wheels, single-colour trim, a full set of instruments and winding windows. But we see two phases of the model – with and without front quarterlights.

Although more common, the later Innocenti 1300 Export is still unusual, especially in Britain, where it was not sold when new. Interior of Innocenti 1300 Export has six-pack instrumentation, while rear end has boot lid adapted to take a square Italian number plate – although this is a British plate on a car that was exported when new to Belgium!

reversing lights, the larger rear window and Italian-made Rostyle-type wheels. The all-synchromesh gearbox appeared on Innocentis in early 1969. From 1970 to 1972, Innocenti's Mini Cooper continued with the 998cc engine but was now called the Mark III, with body modifications similar to the British ADO 20 Mini, including concealed door hinges and winding windows – plus quarterlights from October 1970.

As the Italian home market car tax system always favoured smaller-capacity cars, it was only in 1972 that Innocenti discontinued the 998cc Mini Cooper in favour of a Mini Cooper 1300, fitted with a 1275cc engine in twin-carburettor 71bhp form. This car had rubber cone suspension, a six-dial instrument pack, an alternator and an oil cooler as standard. Radiator grille and badging were changed, and seat trim was now partly in cloth rather than the all-vinyl trim of earlier models.

Shortly after the introduction of the 1300 model, the

Of the new Bertone-designed Mini hatchbacks introduced in 1974, the Mini 120 was the more powerful 1275cc version. Neat and good-looking, both the Mini 90 and 120 models must rank as one of Leyland's missed opportunities – they were simply too expensive compared with small Fiats.

death occurred of company founder Fernando Innocenti, and the family negotiated the sale of the business to British Leyland. Geoffrey Robinson was sent out as managing director of the new subsidiary (later MD of Jaguar, he is now the Labour MP for a Coventry constituency, owner of the *New Statesman*, and a millionaire). He decided to expand Innocenti sales throughout continental Europe and in 1973 added the 1300 Export model, which was also for a time built in BL's assembly factory at Seneffe in Belgium.

The 1300 Export was better equipped and better built than any other Mini Cooper. Its specification included dual-circuit brakes, and reclining seats soon became standard equipment. As it was never made with right-hand drive, it was not sold in Britain, but it was sought-after by Mini Cooper enthusiasts in many European countries. With a claimed top speed of 97.5mph (157kph), it offered traditional Mini Cooper S performance, unlike the contemporary 1275 GT which could only manage 90mph (145kph). The Innocenti 1300 was sold in Switzerland at Sfr 11,450 in 1974, a hefty premium over the British Mini 1275 GT which retailed at Sfr 8,880.

Innocenti introduced the new Bertone-styled three-door hatchback Mini 90 and 120 models in 1974. Although attractive, the new cars were not the hoped-for success, and Innocenti's production dropped disastrously from 60,700 in 1974 to 33,000 in 1975 and 13,800 in 1976. By then Leyland, beset by financial difficulties in Britain, had decided to pull out. Leyland Innocenti went into liquidation in 1975 and was bought by the Italian-Argentinian tycoon Alejandro de Tomaso, already established as a car manufacturer under his own name and also by this time in control of Maserati. He dropped the original Mini but continued production of the Bertone-styled car, in 1982 replacing the A-series engine with a three-cylinder Daihatsu engine. In 1990 he sold his car manufacturing interests to Fiat, and the Innocenti went out of production three years later.

The short-lived Spanish-built AUTHI Mini Cooper, badging and vinyl roof setting it apart from the Innocentis. The interior differed from the British Mini Coopers but was very much like the Innocentis.

AUTHI in Spain..................................

There was also the Spanish connection. In 1966 BMC established a joint venture in Spain under the title Automoviles de Turismo Hispano Ingles, or AUTHI for short, with a factory at Pamplona. The early products were mostly versions of the 1100 range but Minis joined them in 1968. In 1971 AUTHI produced 20,000 cars per year, while the best year was 1973 with total production of over 43,000 cars of which more than 26,000 were Minis; but AUTHI by then also made the Michelotti-restyled Austin 1300, known as the Austin Victoria and originally designed for production in South Africa, where it was called the Austin Apache.

Spanish Mini production started out with a 1275cc model, with a single-carburettor 1275cc engine and a luxury interior. It was only later joined by more basic models with the 998cc and 848cc engines. In 1969 British Leyland bought 51 per cent of the shares held by their Spanish co-operators NMQ, and in 1973 AUTHI became a wholly-owned BLMC subsidiary. By then a 1275 GT model was in production although with a short-nose Mini bodyshell, unlike the British 1275 GT, and in October 1973 the AUTHI Mini Cooper was added. This was largely based on the contemporary Innocenti Mini Cooper 1300 but incorporated many components of Spanish manufacture, such as the electrical equipment, and was available in its own range of single-tone colours, offset by a black vinyl roof – a unique distinction for these cars among Mini Coopers.

Sadly, the success of the Spanish Mini was short-lived. By 1975, AUTHI built fewer than 4000 Minis of a total production of 17,500 cars. As it had done in Italy, Leyland decided to pull out of Spain altogether. Production was stopped before the end of 1975, and the Pamplona factory was eventually sold to General Motors, to play a part in GM's expansion plan for Spain which eventually led to the production of the Opel/Vauxhall Corsa models there from 1982 onwards.

MINI COOPER REBORN

J457 PHP

By 1980, it seemed that the Mini had had its day. BL was bringing out its new small car, the Metro, and the Mini range was drastically pruned, leaving within a couple of years only the basic Mini saloon in production. And from the still respectable 1980 production figure of 150,000 cars, by 1983 it had dropped to just below 50,000. In the latter part of the 1980s Mini production stabilised at around 35,000 cars per year. It was touch and go whether the model might be axed, even though there were still faithful Mini customers at home and abroad who would not buy anything else.

Much of the credit for saving the Mini at this time

The 1.3i production model is the best-known of the highly successful modern Mini Coopers, and was made from 1991 to 1996.

must go to Graham Day, who became chief executive of BL, soon re-named Rover Group, in 1986. He realised that there was still plenty of potential in Britain's best-loved car, and authorised a revitalised marketing campaign with such slogans as 'Minis have feelings too' and 'You never forget your first Mini'. Suddenly potential customers who might have quite forgotten that the Mini was still in production realised that they could still buy a new one – and quite a few did. The Mini also

The 1.3i interior featured bright red carpets and seats trimmed partly in leather. The ignition shield dominates the 1.3i engine bay, and the electronic 'black box' for engine management is on the left.

enjoyed increasing sales in some of the key export markets, most notably Japan where sales shot up from a modest 1000 cars in 1985 to a staggering 12,000 in 1990.

Although France, Germany and Italy also remained good markets for the Mini, this latter-day Japanese love affair with the car was something out of the ordinary, bearing in mind how few other British cars, and indeed how few imported cars altogether, were sold in this market. Why did the Mini suddenly catch on in Japan?

One reason is undoubtedly the Japanese pre-occupation with small cars, and the Mini's particular 'street-cred' with the more sophisticated Japanese car buyer. It is not a retro design but an original. It has the snob value of being imported, but could have been tailor-made for Japanese motoring conditions. It uniquely combines innovation with tradition, and it is a highly individual statement without being in any way outrageous. It is also British, and thus fits right in with the on-going Japanese

The 'Racing' and 'Flame' limited editions of 1989 were the first modern Minis which tried to evoke memories of the 1960s. The introductory model of the Mini Cooper in 1990 was a limited edition which soon became known as the 'Commemorative' model. The bonnet stripes bore facsimiles of John Cooper's signature.

fascination with all things British, from Burberry coats to single malt whiskies. Many of the world's most serious Mini collectors are in Japan, and a surprising number of classic Minis have been exported there from Britain. It is quite an eye-opener looking at the pictures and prices in the classified columns of Japanese motoring magazines!

Meanwhile, back in Britain, the Mini reached its 30th anniversary in 1989. That year saw the first reminders of Mini heritage applied to current production as Minilite-style alloy wheels and white roofs were fitted to the Racing and Flame limited edition models. Cosmetics were one thing, but what about doing a high-performance version of the Mini?

Rover Japan had already approached John Cooper

directly about doing something to revive the legendary Mini Cooper, and a prototype was duly completed with a 1275cc MG Metro engine but fell at the first hurdle when the Rover Group declined the opportunity to manufacture such a car. John Cooper, however, did obtain official approval for a tuning kit for the 998cc Mini which he subsequently exported in quite some numbers to Japan, as well as finding customers in the UK where they were sold through Rover outlets.

There was also the limited-production ERA Mini Turbo, an outside project from ERA at Dunstable but one to which Rover did give its approval. ERA took the standard Mini and fitted the turbocharged 1275cc engine from the MG Metro Turbo, together with 13in alloy wheels, a body kit and a fully re-trimmed interior. At £12,000 this was the most expensive Mini hitherto but buyers were rewarded with a 110mph (177kph) top speed. Of the production run of only 435 cars, a mere 98 were sold in Britain and it is a fair bet that many of the rest found their way to Japan. The ERA Mini Turbo had a short production period, lasting only from 1989 to 1991.

Having watched the introduction of the ERA, John Cooper in 1989 again went to Rover with his proposal for a new 1275cc Mini Cooper, and this time was given a

The regular production model followed later in 1990, with cosmetic differences and less equipment. It still used the carburettor engine. John Cooper, the inspiration behind the modern Mini Cooper, shows off the 1.3i at its 1991 launch at Goodwood.

much warmer reception. The idea was turned over to Rover's new Special Projects department (RSP), and it was agreed to launch a special limited edition of the reborn Mini Cooper in 1990.

The car was to be fitted with the MG Metro 1275cc engine, at this stage still in carburettor form. This 61bhp engine endowed the car with a top speed of 89mph (143kph) – a little slower than the original Cooper S – while 0-60mph (0-96kph) took 11.4sec. Although few other modifications were made from standard Mini specification, which by this time included 12in wheels and servo-assisted front disc brakes, the car was, interestingly enough, from the start fitted with a catalytic converter to the exhaust system – some time ahead of this becoming a legal requirement in Britain but obviously with an eye to export sales in Japan and Germany.

In cosmetic terms, the car was highly specified. A special range of colour schemes all had contrast-colour roofs, and there were Minilite-style alloy wheels, a removable glass sunroof and extra halogen driving lamps. The interior was trimmed partly in leather, following the style of the Mini 30th anniversary Limited Edition. The bonnet had two white stripes each with a facsimile of John Cooper's signature. The price of the RSP Mini Cooper, which went on sale in July 1990, was £6995.

Only 1650 examples of the RSP car were made in

1990 of which 1000 were sold in the UK. Rover had already planned to follow the RSP car with a normal production model, launched in October 1990. To distinguish it from the RSP model, it became known as the 'Mainstream' Mini Cooper, while the RSP model came to be known as the 'Commemorative' model.

By sacrificing some of the extra equipment of the Commemorative model, the Mainstream car could be sold for £6596. It had simpler all-fabric interior trim, it lacked the sunroof and the extra driving lamps, and had no white stripes on the bonnet, apart from other smaller differences. The performance was identical to the Commemorative car. In production for about a year, until October 1991, the Mainstream model reached a

The links with John Cooper have been repeatedly reaffirmed! Here he is again in 1995, still happy to pose for Rover's publicity photographs. The 35th anniversary edition of 1996 was painted Almond Green with a white roof. John Rhodes, tyre-smoking Mini Cooper racing legend of the 1960s, is at the wheel.

total production figure of 19,899 cars – which meant that almost half of all Mini production consisted of Mini Coopers.

The rebirth of the Mini Cooper met with a degree of disbelief, if of a very sympathetic nature, from the motoring press. In a group test in *Car* magazine the inevitable verdict was 'you will either love or hate the Mini' – a rather ancient truism which could have been uttered with equal validity in 1959. The Mini Cooper's sharp and agile handling won praise but the car was considered to be noisy, uncomfortable and slow. L.J.K. Setright was one who leaped to the Mini's defence, praising 'the staunch independence that makes the Mini as refreshing as it always was, and makes it impossible for the others to bear comparison with it'.

For those who enjoyed the new Mini Cooper but

The Mini Cabriolet of 1992: although it shared the Mini Cooper engine, it was not badged as a Mini Cooper.

found it slightly wanting in performance, help was quickly at hand – John Cooper soon offered a twin-carburettor tuning kit to turn the car into an 'S' version, with 78bhp. Rover in 1991 launched its 'Flares, Kinky Boots and Flower Power' campaign, offering three different packs of dealer-fitted options, known as the 'Italian Job', 'RAC Rally' and 'Monte Carlo' packs, which offered some of the items that had been standard on the original Commemorative model – glass sunroof, extra driving lamps and bonnet stripes among them.

In October 1991, the Mini Cooper truly entered modern times, as the 1.3i model was launched with fuel injection and an electronic engine management system. Although the fuel injection system only offered a small increase in power, to 63bhp, torque was up from 91Nm to 95Nm, and top gear acceleration was improved although top speed was only up to 92mph (148kph). Bonnet stripes and driving lamps were re-instated as standard, and there was yet another interior trim scheme, with seats again in part leather.

At £7995 in early 1992, the 1.3i model took the Mini a further step up-market, and continued to account for a large share of overall Mini sales, even though there was an overall decrease in Mini production – down from a remarkable 46,000 in 1990 to 35,000 in 1991 and 26,000 in 1992. Over the following years Mini production stabilised at around 20,000 cars per year. The Mini's success in export markets continued, with typically 75 per cent of production being sold abroad in the early 1990s. To cater for export requirements, especially in Japan, Rover offered the Mini Cooper with automatic transmission – never available in the home market – and also, in 1994, managed to shoe-horn a factory-fitted air conditioning system into the Mini's already well-filled engine compartment.

Further surprises were in store for those who thought the Mini was reaching the end of potential development. While Minis had been converted into cabriolets ever since the early 1960s, when the small independent coachbuilder Crayford in Kent brought out soft-top Minis, no proper factory-built or company-approved Mini convertible had been offered. When this finally happened, the inspiration came from Germany where, in 1991, Rover dealer Lamm Autohaus of Frankfurt modified a batch of 75 such cars that were finished by Rover at Longbridge and sold in the UK. Then at the 1992 International Motor Show at the NEC near Birmingham, Rover launched the factory-built Mini Cabriolet, which shared the Mini Cooper's injection engine although the car was not badged as a Mini Cooper. The car went on sale in the following year with a price tag of almost £12,000. It had luxury touches such as a unique interior, a full-width walnut dashboard and Revolution alloy wheels. At the price, this was for the serious Mini devotee only, but the Cabriolet continued in limited production into 1996.

Non-Cooper Mini models also adopted the 1275cc engine – although in carburettor form with 50bhp – and the catalyst exhaust in 1992. There were now three Mini saloon models – Sprite and Mayfair with the 50bhp engine, and the Mini Cooper – apart from the regular 'limited edition' versions, mostly based on the standard model. The first Mini Cooper based limited edition was the Monte Carlo SE model of 1994, commemorating the 30th anniversary of the first Monte Carlo Rally win for

Paddy Hopkirk (centre), John Brigden (left) and Ron Crellin (right) with the 1960s Monte-winning Minis and the car prepared for the 1994 rally. In 1994 Rover launched the limited edition Monte Carlo version of the Cooper (inset). Tony Dron with his appropriately-registered 1996 Monte Carlo car (below), the first modern Mini to finish this classic rally.

the original Mini Cooper. A total of 200 were made, each costing £7995. This came in red or black, both with a white roof, and a two-tone red/cream interior trim scheme, while the walnut dashboard was the same as used on the Cabriolet. Subsequently, the wood dash and a full leather trim kit became optional on the normal production Mini Coopers. In 1996 there was a further special Mini Cooper, marking the 35th anniversary of the model. Finished in classic Almond Green with a white roof, again only 200 examples were built, and without any advertising they sold out very quickly at £8500 each.

Neither car, however, had any mechanical modifications. Those in search of a faster Mini Cooper could still apply to John Cooper Garages for a tuning kit to turn their car into a Mini Cooper S which, with relatively simple and traditional tuning measures, produced a healthy 83.5bhp: enough to insure a top speed just over the 100mph (161kph) mark and to bring the 0-60mph (0-96kph) time down to a fraction under 10sec. The leather and walnut interior was set off by drilled alloy window winders and door handles.

In mid-1995, the cost of a Cooper-converted car was £9975, although the leather trim was a £985 option. By that time the basic Mini Cooper cost £7695 and, objectively speaking, was no match for a modern small sports saloon such as the Fiat Cinquecento Sporting at £6275, yet the Mini still continued to charm its way into many car buyers' affection.

The new Mini Cooper also 'charmed' its way back into motor sport. John Brigden, long-standing Mini enthusiast, rally driver and marketing consultant to British Motor Heritage, proposed to Rover in 1993 that the new

Evocative publicity shot: Rover's modern marketing skills were used to the full in setting the 1997 Mini Cooper in this nostalgic workshop.

These were the much altered 1997 Minis: the ordinary Mini behind and a Mini Cooper with 'sports pack' equipment at the front.

found sponsorship from, among others, the Japanese classic car importers, Sanwa Trading, and several of the Haymarket Group motoring magazines.

The first rally car was unveiled on the *Autocar* stand at the 1993 London Motor Show, while a test car was constructed at Canterbury Auto Auctions, overseen by Simon Skelton. A new Group A engine, using the single-point fuel injection, was commissioned from well-known Mini competition specialist Bill Richards Racing. Southern Carburettors and Weber Alpha helped out with the engine installation. Paddy Hopkirk, who had won the 1964 Monte Carlo Rally in a Mini Cooper, and his old co-driver Ron Crellin were approached to drive the car, and were delighted to accept. They put in some useful testing in France in December 1993. At the same time, the team was commissioned to build two further vehicles, one for a Swiss competitor, Philippe Camandona, the other for Philippe Chevalier, the Rover dealer of

Mini Cooper should be homologated so that it could take part in the 1994 Monte Carlo Rally. Support for this project came from Kevin Jones of Rover's External Affairs department and from Nikki Darzinskas, Mini brand manager. The company allocated a small budget for the homologation, while Brigden and his partner, Jeremy Coulter, tackled the practicalities. They quickly

Valence in the South of France. A fourth car was built up for none other than Timo Makinen to drive but was sadly stolen only days before the event. The team was able to build a replacement vehicle in a very short time, but this proved to be unreliable and retired after the first stage.

Hopkirk started the first international rally for a Mini for 10 years from Bad Homburg in Germany. Both he and Camandona reached Monte Carlo, placed in the top 50, but Chevalier had retired by this point. Sadly Hopkirk's alternator let him down on the last night, and Camandona was also forced out with electrical problems. But the Mini had proved that it still had potential in modern motor sport. Later in 1994 Russell Brookes took a new car, built by Barratts of Canterbury, on the RAC Rally, finishing sixth in class and 84th overall.

For the 1995 Monte, French driver Andruet drove the only Mini entered, but an accident in the early stages led to mechanical problems which eventually forced him to retire. The Brookes car from the RAC Rally was converted to race specification for the 24-hour race at the Nürburgring in June 1995, the drivers being Brigden, Coulter and Tony Dron. The car finished the race – the first modern Mini to complete a 24-hour event – in 92nd place overall (of 176 starters) and was sixth in class. Minis now also began to appear in the British National Rally Championship, drivers being Daniel Harper (in Group A), John Flynn and Dave Johnson (both in Group N).

So far, no modern Mini had actually finished the Monte Carlo Rally. Brigden was determined that this should be rectified in 1996, as the ultimate revenge over the disqualification exactly 30 years before. The ex-Brookes car was once again prepared, now sporting a new – and appropriate – registration number, D555GRX, specially allocated by the DVLA. The car was entrusted to Dron and co-driver Alistair Douglas. A few

This is the standard interior of the 1997 Mini Cooper but a wide choice of alternative seat trim is available.

early mechanical problems were overcome, and the car finished 69th overall, with only one other Group A car ahead of it. Makinen's 1994 Monte Carlo car was also on this Monte, driven by Keith Bird, who finished as well although further down the list. No fewer than 25 Fiat Cinquecentos ran in the same capacity class, the Dron/Douglas Mini finishing about halfway up a gaggle of Fiats.

The task of continuing the Mini's career in motor sport was then allocated to British Motor Heritage. Two cars were prepared for the Nürburgring 24-hour race but neither finished owing to teething problems. However, in a 6-hour event at the same circuit in August 1996, the cars came first and second in class. The team drivers included Dron and Brigden – the latter the man whose idea had started the programme three years earlier.

On 31 January 1994, much to the surprise of motor industry commentators world-wide, it was announced that Rover Group – owned since 1988 by British Aerospace – would be sold to BMW. At the time it was speculated that one reason BMW wanted to take over Rover was the British company's expertise in building small front-wheel drive cars, while Rover's rich heritage, with the Mini prominent, had also played a role. Maybe there was some truth in the claim made by some Mini enthusiasts that the Mini was so good BMW had to buy the company that made it. One fact which prompted such speculation was that BMW's chairman, Bernd Pischetsrieder, was a relative of the Mini's creator, Sir Alec Issigonis – his grandmother was the sister of Sir Alec's mother.

Over the next couple of years there was increasing media speculation about an all-new Mini, and, as had occurred many times before, the early demise of the original Mini was predicted, owing to the claimed inability of the ageing design to be made to conform to anticipated European automotive mandatory standards for safety, emissions and noise. The crystal-ball gazers must have been very disappointed by two news releases issued by Rover on 1

Mini Coopers of the most recent era have come with more cosmetic permutations than ever before. Options on view here are a chequered roof decal and bonnet stripes, exterior brightwork packs, white accessory alloy wheels, additional lamps and chromed wheelarch spats.

October 1996. One announced the most radical changes for the Mini throughout its 37-year career, and the other confirmed that there would indeed be a new version of the Mini for the next millennium.

The new 1997 Mini was to be available in just two versions, Mini and Mini Cooper, each priced in the UK at £8995 (on the road). Both versions shared a re-designed A-series 1275cc engine, now with multi-point fuel injection and 63bhp. The injection system and a new distributor-less electronic ignition system were controlled by an engine management system originally developed for the MGF VVC and the Rover 800 KV6 engines. A much improved torque curve allowed a much higher 2.76:1 final drive ratio to be fitted, the reduction in engine revs at cruising speed having a beneficial impact on noise levels and economy while leaving performance almost unaffected. In a shock to all Mini traditionalists, the radiator was moved to the front of the car and an electric fan was fitted. The option of automatic transmission was discontinued in European markets.

Combined with the much-modified power train, the Mini was given additional safety features including a driver's airbag and door-mounted side impact protection bars. Both models were well-equipped in standard form, with a walnut dash, better sound insulation, more comfortable front seats and all-new interior trim. Alloy wheels were standard on both models, but with two different designs on Mini and Mini Cooper. The Cooper model still had its contrast-colour roof and bonnet stripes as identification points. Both models now had a new Mini badge, with the word 'MINI' in a winged, green medallion – perceived as a further step towards re-inforcing Mini's unique brand identity with its own values within Rover Group.

It was clearly Rover's strategy to re-position the Mini

further upmarket, distancing it from mass-market competition such as the Fiat Cinquecento, the Renault Twingo (not sold in the UK) and the much-discussed new Ford Ka.

Having learned much from its experience with Minis in Japan and Europe, Rover now indicated, by pulling away from the Mini's previous position as a low-price entry level model, that it saw the Mini increasingly as a fashion statement. Buyers were invited to choose between a Mini and a Mini Cooper simply on the basis of the imagery projected by each model.

There was also a remarkably extensive list of options and accessories that Mini buyers could choose from to personalise their cars. This included the 'Sport Pack' with 13×6J alloy wheels shod with 175/50R13 tyres hiding under wide body-coloured wheelarch spats – which, because of greater drag, actually cut top speed from 90mph (145kph) to 84mph (135kph). There was also a choice of two 'chrome packs', a 'wood pack', an 'alloy pack', a wide range of additional colours – including 1960s favourites such as Almond Green and Surf Blue – and no fewer than six different colours for the optional leather trim. There were five different optional alloy wheels, a choice of sunroofs and, if you really wanted, either a chequered or a Union Jack roof decal.

Never before in the history of the Mini – nor, in all probability, in Rover's history – had such a wide choice of options been offered. Is it a little naughty to suggest that Rover had very quickly learned a lesson from BMW, whose list of options and personalised colour and trim schemes is legendary?

On the road, the improvements to the 1997 Mini were immediately noticeable: the car was so much quieter, while the new gearing allowed top speed to be reached in third gear, with fourth being more in the nature of an overdrive for relaxed motorway cruising. With the improvements to the 1997 Mini, it now seemed certain that the car would continue to meet European legislation until the year 2003, well past its 40th birthday in 1999.

By 2003, the odds are that there will be a new Mini. Rover's other piece of news in October 1996 put an end to some of the speculation about the ultimate replacement for the Mini. There would be a new Mini, it would be built in the UK, and production figures would

The road testers of *Autocar* magazine putting the 1997 Mini Cooper through its paces. The most startling feature of the under-bonnet view of the 1997 Mini is that the radiator is now mounted low down at the front. The window sticker was spotted on an American-owned Mini...

considerably exceed current Mini volumes. And the new car would use a new small engine, to be built in a joint venture between BMW/Rover and Chrysler, in an as yet unnamed South American location, with the same engine being used in future Chrysler products.

Whatever the shape and specification of the Mini to come, it should live up to the brand values for Mini which Rover defines as 'energy, escapism, excitement, individuality and innovation'. The acid test will be whether the new car is instantly recognisable as a Mini, and whether it will appeal to the confirmed enthusiasts – as Rover succeeded brilliantly in doing with the MGF. And will there be a Mini Cooper version of the new car? We will have to wait and see…

THE MINI COOPER TODAY

The original Mini Coopers of the 1960s have long since been sought-after as classic cars. Indeed, their image and reputation have in a sense pulled all the other early Minis along with them, so that any early Mini now has status as a collector's piece – but with the Coopers remaining the most desired, and most expensive, of the different models.

Quite apart from the fact that the Coopers are such charismatic little cars, they have several factors in their favour. They are still perfectly adequate for most types of everyday motoring – with the exception of long motorway journeys which become tiresome. There is a flourishing club scene, with numerous different events. Most spare parts are available: so many parts are shared with other Minis, some even with current models, and there is a growing range of re-manufactured items. Another argument in their favour is that their excellent fuel consumption can make them very cheap to run –

There are Minis of all sorts in this group, including replicas of the 1960s Cooper team racers, gathered by Broadspeed Engineering.

depending on your style of driving! And as production stopped in 1971, even the youngest of the original Coopers qualifies for tax-exempt status in Britain.

Mini Coopers have always attracted the customisers and improvers. Peter Sellers started something when he had Hooper customise his Mini back in the early 1960s at a reputed cost of £1000 – a fabulous sum to spend on a small car in those days. Look through the advertisements in some of the 1960s magazines and you will be dazzled by the selection of accessories and extras it was possible to buy for Mini Coopers, or indeed Minis.

There was an element of cross-breeding at the time, with some owners of lesser Minis wanting to bring their cars up to Mini Cooper specification in looks if not in terms of performance. After all it did not cost much to paint the roof white! Many cars were tuned, and others were given the full customising treatment, notably by Harold Radford whose 'Mini de Ville' was the last word in luxury, with wood and leather, full instrumentation, winding windows and sometimes body modifications such as a sunroof, different headlamps or even a hatchback. Even if not going to such lengths, many Mini or Mini Cooper owners at the time enjoyed personalising their cars, with sports steering wheels, extra instruments, different seats or the new-fangled cast-alloy wheels.

In the 1970s, when new Mini Coopers were not available and the older cars gradually dropped down towards the bottom of the second-hand market, many cars ended up with owners who neglected them. As Mini Coopers became 'bangers', corners were cut. There was little interest in originality, some cars were fitted with later parts, and often with incorrect replacement engines – a wide selection of 1275cc A-series engines was by then available. If the front end of the car was damaged, you could always replace it with a one-piece glass-fibre moulding, and if the original chassis and body number plates were lost, who cared? Those cars which were still being actively used in motor sport sometimes ended up almost unrecognisable.

Now the tide has turned. Customising is more frequently found on later Minis, with most owners and enthusiasts of the 1960s cars more interested in returning their cars to original specification. There is an important exception to this rule: any car that was professionally tuned or customised from new will now most certainly be considered more interesting – and valuable – than a standard car of the same model and year. Most sought-after of all are those cars which have an authenticated competition history, particularly the works rally cars, but also any of the racing cars used by one of the famous teams such as Cooper or Broadspeed.

It would now be a very lucky find to come across an original low-mileage car with a fully documented history. Inevitably, almost all cars have had some work done on them at some stage, and many have been fully restored. The two most important considerations facing anyone looking at a 1960s Mini Cooper with a view to buying it are originality and authenticity. The first is perhaps easier to determine with such a wealth of literature available, including the outstanding *Original Mini Cooper* by John Parnell (published by Bay View Books Ltd) and a useful *Buyer's Guide* booklet by the same author (published by the Mini Cooper Register).

Authenticity is a different matter altogether, and an absolute minefield. There have sadly been many cases of 'fake' cars being passed off by unscrupulous vendors as something that they are not. Sometimes these have been ordinary Mini Coopers masquerading as S models, and others have been created by dressing up non-Cooper Minis. There have been attempts at adapting the identity of works rally cars to vehicles of more humble origin. In some cases, any supporting documentation may well relate to a long-defunct genuine car, and it can become very difficult to sort out the truth. Neither a current DVLA registration document nor a Heritage Production Record Trace Certificate is a guarantee of the authenticity of a certain car, unless supported by other evidence. And the absence of these documents is almost certainly an indicator that there is something suspect about the car in question.

There may also be instances of the same identity having been adapted for more than one car. There is anecdotal evidence that this sort of thing went on almost in the days when the Mini Cooper was still in production. In later years it has perhaps been facilitated by the increasingly world-wide trade in classic cars and the fact that many eager Mini enthusiasts in other countries are less wise to the possibilities of creative interpretation of Mini identities – in fact, a case of innocents abroad.

Setting aside for a moment these vexed questions, what are the problems that you can expect to come across in a Mini Cooper which will, after all, be anything from 25 to 35 years old? Not only their age but some of the features of the body design make Minis particularly prone to corrosion. Almost any area of the bodywork can be affected, from floor to roof. Some of the worst areas are hidden from superficial inspection and the car can look much better than it actually is. The front wings are notorious for rusting through from the inside due to mud being trapped by the headlamp bowls. The triangular door hinge panels and the hinge posts are often equally badly affected, while water leaking in from above can eventually rust out the front floorpans and the crossmember where the seats are attached. At the back of the car, the rear subframe is one of the most common rust areas on any elderly Mini.

Apart from rust, many Minis have suffered accident damage over the years, often poorly repaired with panels badly fitted or, even worse, the whole car slightly out of alignment – something that is immediately obvious if you follow such a car on the road, watching its slightly diagonal progress.

Luckily, body panel availability is excellent, and the

Mini enthusiasm around the world. Seen in Japan (above) is a very original looking Mini Cooper together with a car with a roof chop. Lightly **customised car with small-scale replica (right) lives in Germany, registered to a proud owner from Munich – BMW city!**

main pitfalls lurking for the unwary mainly concern the questions of using the correct type of panel – avoiding, for instance, late-type sill panels with six vent holes when the correct type with four vent holes is available. There are other subtle differences between various models: in particular, the Mark III Mini or ADO 20 model of 1969 onwards had a very much modified body compared with the earlier cars. Where originality is the goal, it always pays to go to a proper Mini specialist rather than rely on a local supplier of pattern panels or even the nearest Rover dealer. Unipart is a wonderful organisation and many of the panels for recent Minis are interchangeable with their 1960s equivalents – the differences may be small but they are sometimes vital.

Many cars have had their engines replaced. Some have genuine BMC Service replacement engines, identified by engine number prefixes starting with the code 8G – but beware. It is the three-figure code immediately after 8G that should be checked out as this is the only means of identifying whether these 'Gold Seal' engines are of the correct type for the car. Some cars have been fitted with engines from other models using transverse A-series engines, in particular 1275cc engines from the BMC 1300 range of 1967-74. These will have prefixes starting with 12H followed by a three-figure code which is *not* 397 or 398, the only correct codes for the Mini Cooper S Mark III.

Of the various engine components, blocks for the 997cc engine and for the various S type engines are scarce to non-existent, and other engine parts unique to the Coopers are not that easy to find, although the later

and better cylinder head casting for the S, with casting number 12G940, is plentiful. The 998cc engine is very similar to the single-carburettor version used in the Hornet/Elf range from 1963, and in the ordinary Minis from 1967 onwards, and it is really only the pistons which are difficult to find. One particular consideration which will become ever more important is the question of using unleaded fuel – this is possible but only if the cylinder head has been modified with hardened valve seats, and such conversions are now available.

Mini gearboxes are subject to more than normal wear and tear owing to the fact that they share the engine oil supply. Only the very earliest Mini Coopers have the cone-type synchromesh, which was frankly lamentable, and it is unlikely that very many of these gearboxes have survived. The 1962-68 gearboxes had more adequate baulk-ring synchromesh, which is more reliable but was still not fitted to first gear. Parts for all the three-synchro gearboxes are becoming more difficult to find. The all-synchro 'box used from October 1968 is a much better proposition especially for drivers used to modern-day gearboxes, and parts are much easier to find.

Of the various chassis parts, potentially the biggest problem concerns the Hydrolastic suspension fitted from 1964 to 1971. Hydrolastic is now a superseded technology, with parts and service know-how in increasingly short supply. The displacer units and their connecting pipes need to be watched for leaks, and it is not uncommon to see a Hydrolastic-suspended car with the suspension on one side in a state of near-collapse. Some cars which originally had Hydrolastic have been converted to the more reliable and almost maintenance-free solid rubber cone suspension – the subframes are different but interchangeable.

One of the biggest Mini events ever was the 30th birthday party hosted by Rover at Silverstone in August 1989.

One area that is often a major concern when looking at an unrestored classic car is the condition of the interior trim. Original trim parts which were never much in demand during the first service life of a car are among the first to be jettisoned by the manufacturer once a model has gone out of production. The Mini Cooper owner seeking to re-trim a car used to face this problem, but in recent years demand has thankfully made it possible for most of the interior trim parts to be re-manufactured by specialist suppliers, to as near original specification as is possible. One suspects that the greatest demand is for the classic combination of Tartan Red and Gold/Grey brocade…

Which, then, is the best Mini Cooper to go for? This depends on personal preference, coupled with which cars are available, in what condition and at which prices. Most common are the 998cc models, which make fine cars for all-round enjoyment; a 998cc version may not have quite the performance of the 1275cc S but it does not do too badly, and there is quite a difference in price between the two. It is probably the simplest model to find parts for. The late Mark II models have the advantage of the fully-synchronised gearbox, but on the other hand you might prefer the solid suspension found only on the very early 1964 998cc cars.

The 1275cc is the most common of the S models. It offers a more exhilarating drive, with not much of a penalty in running costs. Of the 1275cc models, the Mark III of 1970-71 is a little overlooked, with its single-tone colours and rather plain interior not having the same appeal as the colourful Mark Is – but do not turn your nose up at one of these cars which come with built-in rarity.

Other versions are also quite rare. Many of the early 997cc cars and the original 1071cc S models went to breakers' yards before the Mini Cooper acquired cult status. They each present their own particular spare parts problems, and, other than being rare, do not really offer any great advantage over the later models. The ultimate Mini Cooper to many enthusiasts is the 970cc S model, with its unique aura as a racing-orientated 'homologation special', and its undoubted scarcity. While it is a little more temperamental than the others, it is by no means a difficult car to live with, to use or to enjoy.

If it is simply the look of the thing that you like, and you do not want to worry about where the parts are going to come from, help is at hand from Broadspeed Engineering (no relation to the original 1960s racing team; the modern company simply adopted the name), which will take any Mini, even a recent model, and transform it to look like a Mark I Cooper – two-tone colour and trim, the correct grille and badges, and the correct instruments. No deception is intended as these cars retain their original identities for legal and registration purposes. These look-alikes are building up a following and is it any wonder that many orders are coming in from Japan in particular?

It could be argued that Rover to a degree has followed a similar path with its modern Mini Coopers which deliberately play on the nostalgia for the original cars. The Mini Coopers from 1990 onwards have yet to acquire status as true classics, and a prospective purchaser should probably only consider them as he or she would any other fairly recent second-hand car. However, the rare 1990 'Commemorative' Limited Edition model already has a following of its own, as will assuredly the later special versions.

For the future, it is good to see that there is absolutely no sign of Mini-mania abating. Back in 1959, nobody associated with the Mini, whether Alec Issigonis or anybody else, realised quite what they had started but it is still going on and long may it continue to do so!

APPENDIX

Production figures...........................

The production figures quoted below are based on those compiled by John Parnell of the Mini Cooper Register for his book *Original Mini Cooper* (Bay View Books, 1993), with the addition of 300 cars (998cc models built in 1964) which have subsequently been discovered in the records. However, these figures omit CKD cars from 1967 onwards as, by then, CKD cars can no longer be identified in the Longbridge-sourced production records.

997cc	Austin	Morris	Total
1961	912	863	1775
1962	7159	6805	13964
1963	4318	4775	9093
1964	6	22	28
Total	12395	12465	24860

998cc Mark I	Austin	Morris	Total
1963	276	326	602
1964	4529	4314	8843
1965	4236	4027	8263
1966	5857	8836	14693
1967	2939	4324	7263
Total	17837	21827	39664

998cc Mark II	Austin	Morris	Total
1967	881	604	1485
1968	4517	3620	8137
1969	3770	3004	6774
Total	9168	7228	16396

S 1071cc	Austin	Morris	Total
1963	913	826	1739
1964	1222	1070	2292
Total	2135	1896	4031

S 970cc	Austin	Morris	Total
1964	415	430	845
1965	66	52	118
Total	481	482	963

S 1275cc Mark I	Austin	Morris	Total
1964	1318	1108	2426
1965	2384	2603	4987
1966	1691	2412	4103
1967	1096	1701	2797
Total	6489	7824	14313

S 1275cc Mark II	Austin	Morris	Total
1967	292	404	696
1968	1041	1725	2766
1969	1275	1447	2722
1970	79	66	145
Total	2687	3642	6329

S 1275cc Mark III (estimated figures)	
1970	749
1971	821
Total	1570

Overall production figures

Mark I, 997cc and 998cc models	64524
Mark I, all S models	19307
All Mark I models	**83831**
Mark II, 998cc	16396
Mark II, S 1275cc	6329
All Mark II models	**22725**
Mark III, S 1275cc	1570
Grand total, all Mini Coopers	**108126**

(of which **27206** S models)

The desirable Cooper S in Austin-badged 1275cc Mark I form – 6489 of these cars, and 7824 Morris versions, were built between 1964-67. The colour is Tartan Red with Black roof.

75

An alternative set of figures are those 'official' figures which were compiled by BMC at the time, and which include CKD production. There are also other slight variations from Parnell's figures. In the tables below, both sets of figures are quoted for comparison, first for the Mark I and Mark II models:

| BMC | 997/998cc | | S models | |
	Austin	Morris	Austin	Morris
1961	863	781	0	0
1962	7283	6633	0	0
1963	5338★	5008	★	770
1964	4546	4683	3020	2659
1965	4267	4002	2359	2591
1966	5637	8493	1673	2338
1967	4375	8727	1407	2489
1968	4756	9911	1174	2527
1969	4276	9702	985	2126
1970	0	0	?	?
Total	**41341**	**57940**	**10618**	**15500**
	——— 99281 ———		——— 26118 ———	
	——— 125399 ———			

★ For 1963, the Austin S figure was included with Austin 997/998cc models.

| PARNELL | 997/998cc | | S models | |
	Austin	Morris	Austin	Morris
1961	912	863	0	0
1962	7159	6805	0	0
1963	4594	5101	913	826
1964	4535	4336	2955	2608
1965	4236	4027	2450	2655
1966	5857	8836	1691	2412
1967	3820	4928	1388	2105
1968	4517	3620	1041	1725
1969	3770	3004	1275	1447
1970	0	0	79	66
Total	**39400**	**41520**	**11792**	**13844**
	——— 80920 ———		——— 25636 ———	
	——— 106556 ———			

The discrepancy of almost 19,000 cars between the two sets of figures is believed to be accounted for by CKD kits, mainly for Italy (Innocenti) and Australia, from 1967 onwards. A similar discrepancy exists for the Mark III figures of 1970-71, as follows:

BMC (assembled and CKD cars)

	Home	Export	Total
1970	374	9062	9436
1971	418	9657	10057
Total	**792**	**18719**	**19511**

PARNELL (assembled cars only)

	Total
1970	749
1971	821
Total	**1570**

The difference here, of almost 18,000 cars for the two years, is believed to be made up of the CKD kits for Innocenti.

Identification

The car number, often known as the chassis number or Vehicle Identification Number, is the most important number for identification.

These numbers are prefixed by identification codes which are different for Austin and Morris versions, and for Mark I, Mark II and Mark III models, but the same for 997/998cc models and all S models. The following different codes are found:

Mark I	C-A2S7 (Austin)	K-A2S4 (Morris)
Mark II	C-A2SB (Austin)	K-A2S6 (Morris)
Mark III	XAD1	

Note: Mark I and Mark II codes may be followed by the letter L on left-hand drive cars.

All Mark I and Mark II models have car numbers issued in the sequence that was also used for all other Minis built at Longbridge from 1959 to 1969/70. The following are the starting and finishing numbers for the various models, and their production periods:

Model	Car numbers	Production period
Austin 997cc	138301-555232	Jul 61 to Apr 64
Morris 997cc	138311-522751	Jul 61 to Jan 64
Austin 998cc Mk I	486096-1068160	Nov 63 to Sep 67
Morris 998cc Mk I	481251-1064876	Nov 63 to Sep 67
Austin S 1071cc	384101-563570	Jan 63 to Aug 64
Morris S 1071cc	384601-563513	Mar 63 to Aug 64
Austin S 970cc	549501-549992	Jun 64 to Apr 65
Morris S 970cc	550501-550980	Jun 64 to Apr 65
Austin S 1275cc Mk I	551501-1066319	Feb 64 to Sep 67
Austin S 1275cc Mk I	552501-1066320	Feb 64 to Sep 67
Austin 998cc Mk II	1068151-1370956	Sep 67 to Nov 69
Morris 998cc Mk II	1068197-1365476	Sep 67 to Nov 69
Austin S 1275cc Mk II	1068451-1375331	Sep 67 to Feb 70
Morris S 1275cc Mk II	1068471-1375346	Sep 67 to Feb 70
Mini Cooper S Mk III	34127-458987★	Mar 70 to Jun 71

★ The Mark III model had chassis numbers from the new sequence of numbers introduced for the face-lifted Mini (ADO 20) series in 1969.

Many Mini Coopers, including all Mark II and Mark III models, have a suffix letter A after the car number. This indicates that they were built in the Austin factory at Longbridge. Some overseas-built cars – including Innocentis, Authis and Australian cars – have their own individual chassis number series.

Of the other numbers found on the cars, the engine number gives a better identification of whether the car is a Mini Cooper or a Mini Cooper S, and of the different models – always assuming that the engine is original and the engine number has not been tampered with!

The following are the most important engine number prefixes and engine number series:

Engine type		Prefix	Engine numbers
997cc		9F-Sa-H/L	101-28950
998cc	early cars	9FA-Sa-H/L	101-4999
	later cars with positive crankcase ventilation	9FD-Sa-H/L	101-38079
	1968-69 with all-synchro gearbox	9FD-Xe-H/L	101-4423
	1969 models with dynamo	99H-377-C-H/L	} 101-5829
	1969 models with alternator	99H-378-C-H/L	
970cc		9F-Sa-X★	29001-30029
1071cc		9F-Sa-H★★	19201-20410
			26501-34009
1275cc	1964-1968 with three-synchro gearbox	9F-Sa-Y★★★	31001 51397
	1968-1969/70 with all-synchro gearbox	9F-Xe-H	51501-55234
	Mark III with dynamo	12H-397-F	} 101-1700
	Mark III with alternator	12H-398-F	(approx)

★ 970cc engine may also have prefix 9FD-Sa-X or 9FE-Sa-X
★★ 1071cc engine may also have prefix 9FD-Sa-H
★★★ 1275cc engine may also have prefix 9FD Sa Y or 9FE-Sa-Y

All 997cc and 998cc engines may be found in either high-compression or low-compression variations, indicated by the final letter H or L in the prefix. All engine number series and prefixes were shared between Austin and Morris models but the Innocenti and Authi engines had their own number series and prefixes.

The body numbers may be in one of three series, for Mark I, Mark II and Mark III models respectively. Mark I body numbers are prefixed with the letter A and up to three zeroes, and are stamped on a tag on the bonnet-locking platform. These numbers ran in a sequence from 101 to approximately 66247. On Mark II models body numbers are prefixed with the code 250S; they start from 101 and the finishing number is estimated to be around 23000. Mark III body numbers are prefixed with the code B20D, and run from 101 to approximately 1700. CKD kit cars were typically not issued with body numbers.

Commission numbers are found only on Mark II and Mark III models, on a plate with a red border on the right-hand flitch panel in the engine compartment, or on the bonnet-locking platform. Mark II commission numbers run from 101 to an estimated high of 23000; they are prefixed with the code 2-50S and suffixed A. On the Mark III models the commission numbers are prefixed N20D and are again suffixed A; they run from 101 to approximately 1668-1670. Commission numbers were again typically not issued to CKD cars. On Mark II models there is no difference between commission numbers for 998cc models and 1275cc S models.

Finally, the so-called 'front end assembly number'. This number is prefixed FE and is found on a tag on the shroud above the radiator. This number confirms that the car is a Mini (!) but the FE sequence of numbers is shared between all types of Minis built between 1959 and at least 1976, so these numbers cannot be used to confirm that a car is a Mini Cooper. They are not quoted in the production records either, so it is not possible to trace an individual car just from the FE number.

Colour schemes

Mark I

Body	Roof	Trim	Period
Surf Blue	Old English White	Powder Blue/ Silver Brocade	1961-62
Surf Blue	Old English White	Powder Blue/ Gold Brocade	1962-65
Island Blue	Old English White	Cumulus Grey/ Gold Brocade	1965-67
Almond Green	Dove Grey	Porcelain Green/ Dove Grey	1961
Almond Green	Old English White	Porcelain Green/ Dove Grey	1961-67
Smoke Grey	Old English White	Dark Grey/ Dove Grey	1961-64
Tweed Grey	Old English White	Dark Grey/ Dove Grey	1964-67
Tartan Red	Black	Tartan Red/ Gold Brocade	1961-67
Old English White	Dove Grey	Tartan Red/ Gold Brocade	1961
Old English White	Black	Tartan Red/ Gold Brocade	1961-67
Fiesta Yellow	Old English White	Powder Blue/ Silver Brocade	1961-62
Fiesta Yellow	Old English White	Powder Blue/ Gold Brocade	1962-65

Notes A few cars were finished in monotone colours, typically using the main body colour, but also in black. Police cars were finished in Police White with monotone red trim. The works rally cars were Tartan Red with Old English White roofs which were specially repainted by the Competitions Department.

Mark II

Body	Roof	Trim
El Paso Beige	Snowberry White	Black
Sandy Beige	Snowberry White	Black
Island Blue	Snowberry White	Black
Almond Green	Snowberry White	Black
Tartan Red	Black	Black
Snowberry White	Black	Black

Notes A small number of early Mark II cars had Mark I-style two-tone brocade trim or monotone trim in colours other than black, using trim colours from ordinary Minis of the time. Early Mark IIs used Old English White rather than Snowberry White. A few cars were finished in monotone colours including Black, and Police White on Police cars, while some later cars were painted in Mark III monotone colours.

Mark III

Paint	Trim
Antelope (beige)	Black or Icon Red
Bedouin (beige)	Autumn Leaf
Blue Royale	Galleon Blue
Teal Blue	Limeflower or Navy
Blaze (orange)	Navy
Flame Red	Autumn Leaf, Black, Navy or Geranium
Aqua (turquoise)	Black or Navy
Glacier White	Black, Geranium, Navy or Icon Red
Bronze Yellow	Black or Navy

Note Monotone colours only.

Cars built or assembled overseas (including Australian models, as well as the Innocentis and Authis) usually had their own range of colour schemes. Australian cars were usually two-tone, as the UK-built cars, but monotone Black was a regular colour and trim was always monotone. Innocentis were always two-tone but had monotone interior trim. Authis were painted monotone colours but always had a black vinyl roof, while their interior trim was similar to Innocentis.

Technical specifications.....................

MINI COOPER 997cc (1961-64)

Engine Transverse in-line four-cylinder **Construction** Cast-iron block and head **Crankshaft** Three main bearings **Bore × stroke** 62.43mm × 81.28mm (2.46in × 3.20in) **Capacity** 997cc (60.84cu in) **Valves** Overhead valves operated by push-rods **Compression ratio** 9:1 (optional low compression, 8.3:1) **Fuel system** Two SU HS2 (1.25in) carburettors **Maximum power** 55bhp at 6000rpm (low compression, 52bhp at 6000rpm) **Maximum torque** 54.5lb ft (7.53mkg) at 3600rpm (low compression, 53lb ft [7.32mkg] at 3500rpm) **Transmission** Four-speed gearbox in engine sump, 2nd to 4th synchronised, final drive via helical spur gears to front wheels, remote control floor gearchange **Final drive ratio** 3.765:1 **Top gear mph per 1000rpm** 14.9mph (24kph) **Brakes** Lockheed hydraulic, discs front, drums rear **Front suspension** Independent with transverse links of unequal length, rubber springs and hydraulic telescopic shock absorbers **Rear suspension** Independent with trailing arms, rubber springs and hydraulic telescopic shock absorbers **Steering** Rack and pinion **Wheels/tyres** 3.5×10 steel disc wheels, 5.20-10 Dunlop Gold Seal cross-ply tyres **Length** 120.25in (3054mm) **Wheelbase** 80in (2032mm) **Width** 55.5in (1410mm) **Height** 53in (1346mm) **Front track** 48.5in (1232mm) **Rear track** 46in (1168mm) **Unladen weight** 1315lb (597kg) **Gross vehicle weight** 2004lb (910kg) **Top speed** 85mph (137kph) **0-60mph** 17-18sec **Standing ¼-mile** 21sec **Typical fuel consumption** 27-35mpg (10.6-8.2 L/100km)

MINI COOPER S 1071cc (1963-64)

As 997cc model, except: **Bore × stroke** 70.64mm × 68.26mm (2.78in × 2.69in) **Capacity** 1071cc (65.36cu in) **Compression ratio** 9:1 **Maximum power** 70bhp at 6200rpm **Maximum torque** 62lb ft (8.58mkg) at 4500rpm **Transmission** Close-ratio gearbox optional **Final drive ratio** 3.444:1 optional **Top gear mph per 1000rpm** 14.69mph (23.6kph) with standard ratio **Brakes** Vacuum servo added **Wheels/tyres** Ventilated disc wheels, 4.5×10 wheels optional; 5.00L-10 Dunlop C41 cross-ply or 145-10 Dunlop SP radial ply tyres **Front and rear track** Increased by 1in (25mm) when wider wheels fitted **Unladen weight** 1425lb (647kg) **Top speed** 95mph (153kph) **0-60mph** 13sec **Standing ¼-mile** 19sec **Typical fuel consumption** 27-30mpg (10.5-9.4 L/100km)

MINI COOPER 998cc (1964-69)

As 997cc model, except: **Bore × stroke** 64.58mm × 76.2mm (2.54in × 3.00in) **Capacity** 998cc (60.90cu in) **Compression ratio** Optional low compression 7.8:1 **Maximum power** 55bhp at 5800rpm **Maximum torque** 57lb ft (7.88mkg) at 3000rpm (low compression, 56lb ft [7.74mkg] at 2900rpm) **Transmission** All-synchromesh gearbox from Oct 68 **Top gear mph per 1000rpm** 14.7mph (23.7kph) **Front and rear suspension** Interconnected Hydrolastic elements with rear helper coil springs from Sep 64 **Wheels/tyres** 145-10 Dunlop SP radial tyres standard from Mar 64 **Unladen weight** 1359lb (617kg); Mark II from Oct 67, 1432lb (650kg) **Gross vehicle weight** Mark II from Oct 67, 2112lb (959kg) **Top speed** 89mph (143kph) **0-60mph** 14.8sec **Standing ¼-mile** 20sec **Typical fuel consumption** 31.5mpg (9 L/100km)

MINI COOPER S 970cc (1964-65)

As 1071cc model, except: **Bore × stroke** 70.64mm × 61.91mm (2.78in × 2.44in) **Capacity** 970cc (59.19cu in) **Compression ratio** 10:1 **Maximum power** 65bhp at 6500rpm **Maximum torque** 55lb ft (7.60mkg) at 3500rpm **Final drive ratio** 3.765:1 optional ratios: 3.938, 4.133 and 4.267:1 **Front and rear suspension** Interconnected Hydrolastic elements with rear helper coil springs from Sep 64 **Wheels/tyres** 145-10 Dunlop SP radial tyres standard **Top speed** Estimated 92mph (148kph)

MINI COOPER S 1275cc (1964-71)

As 970cc model, except: **Bore × stroke** 70.64mm × 81.33mm (2.78in × 3.20in) **Capacity** 1275cc (77.80cu in) **Compression ratio** 9.75:1 **Maximum power** 75bhp at 5800rpm **Maximum torque** 80lb ft (11.06mkg) at 3000rpm **Transmission** All-synchromesh gearbox from Oct 68 **Final drive ratio** 3.444:1 optional ratios: 3.765, 3.938, 4.133 and 4.267:1 **Top gear mph per 1000rpm** 16.05mph (25.8kph) **Unladen weight** 1435lb (651kg); Mark II and Mark III models, 1537lb

(698kg) **Gross vehicle weight** 2154lb (978kg); Mark II, 2238lb (1016kg); Mark III, 2216lb (1006kg) **Top speed** 97mph (156kph) **0-60mph** 11sec **Standing ¼-mile** 18sec **Typical fuel consumption** 28-34mpg (10-8.3 L/100km)

INNOCENTI MINI COOPER (1966-72)

As 998cc model, except: **Compression ratio** 9:1; Mark II and III from 1968, 9.5:1 **Maximum power** 56bhp at 5800rpm; Mark II/III, 60bhp at 6000rpm **Maximum torque** 57.9lb ft (8mkg) at 3000rpm; Mark II/III, 61.5lb ft (8.5mkg) at 3000rpm **Transmission** All-synchromesh gearbox from 1969 **Brakes** Servo fitted as standard **Front and rear suspension** Hydrolastic **Wheels/tyres** 145SR-10 tyres, 4.5×10 wheels; ventilated disc wheels on Mark I, Rostyle-type wheels on Mark II and III **Front track** 49in (1245mm) **Rear track** 47.6in (1210mm) **Unladen weight** 1476lb (670kg) **Gross vehicle weight** 2181lb (990kg) **Top speed** 90mph (145kph) **0-100kph** 15sec **Typical fuel consumption** 36.7mpg (7.7 L/100km) (NB: Performance data as quoted by Innocenti)

INNOCENTI MINI COOPER 1300, 1300 EXPORT (1972-76)

As Mini Cooper S 1275, except: **Maximum power** 71bhp at 5800rpm **Maximum torque** 79.6lb ft (11mkg) at 3200rpm **Transmission** All-synchromesh gearbox **Front and rear suspension** Independent, with rubber springs and shock absorbers **Wheels/tyres** Rostyle-type 4.5×10 wheels **Front track** 49in (1245mm) **Rear track** 47.6in (1210mm) **Unladen weight** 1520lb (690kg) **Gross vehicle weight** 2225lb (1010kg) **Top speed** 95-97.5mph (153-157kph) **0-60mph** 12.4sec **Typical fuel consumption** 29.2-33.6mpg (9.7-8.4 L/100km) (NB: Technical specifications for the AUTHI Mini Cooper, 1973-75, are similar to the Innocenti Mini Cooper 1300)

MINI COOPER, carburettor engine (1990-91)

As Mini Cooper S 1275, except: **Compression ratio** 10.1:1 **Fuel system** Single SU HIF 44 carburettor **Maximum power** 61bhp at 5500rpm **Maximum torque** 91Nm at 3000rpm **Transmission** All-synchromesh gearbox **Final drive ratio** 3.105:1 **Top gear mph per 1000rpm** 19.6mph (31.5kph) **Brakes** Dual circuits **Front and rear suspension** Independent, with rubber springs and shock absorbers **Wheels/tyres** 4.50B×12 cast-alloy wheels, 145/70SR-12 tyres **Wheelbase** 80.1in (2035mm) **Height** 53.25in (1353mm) **Front track** 48.8in (1240mm) **Rear track** 47.4in (1204mm) **Unladen weight** 1531lb (695kg) **Gross vehicle weight** 2203lb (1000kg) **Top speed** 92mph (148kph) **0-60mph** 11.2sec **Typical fuel consumption** 30-45mpg (9.4-6.3 L/100km)

MINI COOPER 1.3i, fuel injection engine (1991-96)

As carburettor model, except: **Compression ratio** 10.5:1 (low compression for some export markets, 9.4:1) **Fuel system** Single-point (throttle body) fuel injection **Maximum power** 63bhp at 5700rpm (low compression, 53bhp at 5000rpm) **Maximum torque** 95Nm at 3900rpm (low compression, 92Nm at 2600rpm) **Transmission** Automatic gearbox optional in Japan **Final drive ratio** 3.21:1 **Top gear mph per 1000rpm** 18mph (29kph) **Wheels/tyres** Alternative tyre size, 165/60R-12; optional wheels: 6J×13 with 175/50R-13 tyres **Width** 60in (1520mm) when fitted with wider wheels **Front track** 52.2in (1325mm) with wider wheels **Rear track** 49.4in (1254mm) with wider wheels

MINI COOPER, 1997 model (1996 onwards)

As 1.3i model, except: **Fuel system** Twin point fuel injection **Maximum power** 63bhp at 5500rpm **Maximum torque** 95Nm at 3000rpm **Final drive ratio** 2.76:1 **Top gear mph per 1000rpm** 21mph (33.8kph) **Unladen weight** 1575-1586lb (715-720kg); 'sport pack' version, 1608lb (730kg) **Top speed** 90mph (145kph); 'sport pack' version, 84mph (135kph) **0-60mph** 12.2sec; 'sport pack' version, 12.8sec **Standing ¼ mile** 18.9sec; 'sport pack' version, 19.2sec **Typical fuel consumption** 43mpg (6.6 L/100km) (NB: Performance data as quoted by Rover. 'Sport pack' version is fitted with 6J×13 cast-alloy wheels, 175/50R-13 tyres, and wheelarch extensions.)

Notes All technical specifications are based partly on the manufacturer's own literature, but also on contemporary magazine reports and the annual catalogue issue of *Automobil Revue* (Bern, Switzerland). Power and torque figures are as quoted at the time, and are mostly net figures. Performance figures are from various sources, including *The Autocar/Autocar* and *The Motor/Motor*, but some manufacturer's figures are quoted. Fuel consumption figures in mpg are calculated per imperial gallon.

ACKNOWLEDGEMENTS

Grateful thanks are due to the owners whose cars feature in special colour photography by Maurice Rowe, Tony Baker, Neill Bruce and Paul Debois: they are Dave Davies (Morris Cooper MkI), Roy Gudge (Morris Cooper MkII), Simon Empson (Austin Cooper S MkI), Steve Smith (Austin Cooper S MkII), Gordon Peck (Mini Cooper S MkIII) and John Ansing (Innocenti 1300 Export). Other photographs have been sourced from the British Motor Industry Heritage Trust, Rover Group, David Hodges, *Classic & Sports Car* magazine, LAT Photographic, Neill Bruce (including the Peter Roberts Collection), John Parnell, Broadspeed Engineering, John Cooper, British Film Institute, Merseyside Police, *Autocar* magazine, Peter Marti, Joan Sastre, Anders Ditlev Clausager and Mark Hughes. Thanks also to David Hodges for his contribution to the picture research. Valuable input to the chapter about the modern Mini Cooper was provided by John Brigden (details of the car's motor sport exploits) and Kevin Jones of Rover Group Product Communications (information about the production models).